MESSIAH?

Jesus

Simon and Christopher Danes

LION EDUCATIONAL

FOR CATHERINE AND DUVESSA

Text copyright © 1991 Simon and Christopher Danes
This edition copyright © 1991 Lion Publishing plc

Published by
Lion Publishing plc
Sandy Lane West, Oxford, England
ISBN 0 7459 1943 X
Albatross Books Pty Ltd
PO Box 320, Sutherland, NSW 2232, Australia
ISBN 0 7324 0490 8

First edition 1991
Reprinted 1993

Acknowledgments

The authors would like to thank Brian O'Higgins and Paul Bruxby for
their generous hospitality while they were writing.

Where quotations are taken directly from the Bible, the translation
used, by kind permission, is The Good News Bible, copyright 1966, 1971
and 1976 American Bible Society, published by The Bible Societies and Collins.
The quotation on page 68 is from the Revised Standard Version.

Photographs
Allsport (UK) Ltd, page 126 (Akabusi); Howard Barlow, page 110; Barnaby's
Picture Library, page 109 /George Sturm, page 70 (above left); Werner Braun,
page 108 (below); Colchester Museums, page 85; Coventry Cathedral, page 70
(above right); EMI Records (UK) Ltd/Paul Cox, page 126 (Cliff Richard); The
Genesis Project, cover, pages 5, 8, 18, 21, 24, 29, 38, 42, 57, 61, 66, 70
(below), 73, 77, 80, 87, 92, 96, 101, 105, 108 (above), 113, 115, 123, 127;
Sonia Halliday Photographs, page 116; Lion Publishing/David Alexander, pages
45, 120 /Gerald Rogers, page 58 /David Townsend, page 126 (nurse); Mansell
Collection, page 30; News Limited (Australia), page 65; Iain Tait, page 118

Illustrations, maps and graphics
Synagogue, page 10 and Temple, page 50, Maggie Brand; prodigal son, page 51,
Carolyn Cox; good Samaritan, page 84, Tony Morris; seeds, page 91, Laura Potter

Cartoons and picture-strip on pages 22, 27, 33, 40, 48, 49, 62, 64, 81, 94, 95, David Mostyn

Maps, graphics and all other illustrations, Tony Cantale Graphics

Design by Tony Cantale Graphics

The publishers would like to acknowledge the special help of The Genesis
Project in the preparation of this book. A video of the film from which
the photographs have been taken is available from International Films, The
Coach House, Drayton Green, London W13 OJD

British Library CIP applied for

Printed and bound in Malta by Interprint Limited

CONTENTS

* Chapter numbers followed by an asterisk indicate supplementary material which may be omitted if time is limited.

Starting-points

Jesus was born in about 4BC in a small country called Palestine on the edge of the Roman Empire. He worked as a carpenter in a town called Nazareth.

Jesus was a Jew. The Jewish people had suffered under many foreign rulers. They were waiting—waiting for God to save them; waiting for him to send a great leader whom they called the *Messiah*.

When Jesus was about thirty he gave up his job. He became a

What was it that drew people to Jesus, crowding to hear him everywhere he went, forcing him on this occasion to speak from a fisherman's boat on Lake Galilee?

wandering preacher. People flocked to hear him, and some followed him wherever he went.

Who was he? Was he the one they were expecting? Or was he an imposter? Not everyone was on his side. In less than three years he was tried and executed. His enemies had won—or so it seemed.

But that was not the end of the story. His followers became convinced that he had risen from death. They said he was indeed the Messiah—and someone even greater. Thirty years after his execution, the news about him had spread through the Roman Empire. Four books were written about his life. They are the Gospels of Mark, Matthew, Luke and John. Even today, they tell us most of what we know about him.

In this book we shall be exploring Jesus' life and its meaning. What did he teach, and what did it mean? What did he do? And—most important of all—what was it about him that stirred up such violent reactions?

How Did Jesus See His Work?

'The Spirit of the Lord is upon me': Jesus reads Isaiah's prophetic words in the synagogue at Nazareth at the beginning of his public ministry.

Luke's Gospel tells a story about the early days of Jesus' teaching. It helps us to understand how Jesus saw his work.

Jesus had been away from home for some time, teaching in the towns and villages around Galilee. (This is the northern part of Palestine: look at the map.) A lot of people there had listened to him, and he had become famous. All sorts of rumours came back to Nazareth, where he had been brought up.

When Jesus returned home, he went to the synagogue on the Sabbath. There was probably an extra-large congregation. People would have been puzzled by the rumours they had heard. They wanted to find out what they were all about.

Any Jewish man could be asked to read a lesson during the service. This is what Jesus was asked to do. They were keen to hear what he had to say.

Jesus chose a reading from the prophet Isaiah. (The Book of Isaiah is in the Old Testament, the Jewish Bible.) This is what he read:

> 'The Spirit of the Lord is upon me, because he has chosen me to bring good news to the poor.
> He has sent me to proclaim liberty to the captives
> and recovery of sight to the blind,
> to set free the oppressed
> and announce that the time has come when the Lord will save his people.'

5
Saying **the time has come** when God will save his people

1
Bringing **good news to the poor**

HOW DID JESUS SEE HIS WORK?

4
Setting free the oppressed
(those who are treated badly or unjustly)

2
Proclaiming **liberty to the captives**
(setting people free)

3
Giving **sight to the blind**

Copy this diagram. You might like to make this into a poster, using pictures and articles from magazines and newspapers.

Then he said, 'This passage of scripture has come true today.' Jesus meant that the reading is about him.

Let's put this in a diagram.

Luke goes on to tell us how the people reacted to what Jesus said in the synagogue. You might expect them to be pleased at all this good news. At first, they were very surprised. But soon their surprise turned to anger. They dragged

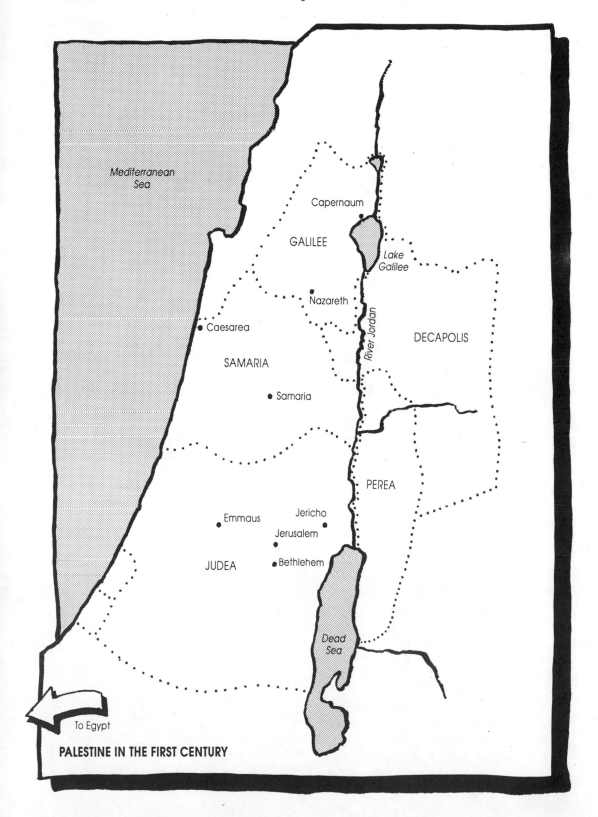

PALESTINE IN THE FIRST CENTURY

Jesus outside and tried to kill him, but he escaped. Why do you think they did this?

It seems strange, but think about it. Suppose a boy from your class or school goes away for a while, someone you have known since you were very young. When he comes back, he begins to say that he is somebody special, and tells you how to live your life. How would you react?

So Jesus brings good news, but many people do not seem to want it. This is going to be the pattern for the rest of his life.

Look at the diagram again. The five things Jesus talks about add up to *good news*—and that is what the word 'gospel' means. Luke tells us about them

Write out the following passage and fill in the missing words from the list below.

Jesus had been preaching around_____.
He went home to_____. On the
_____, he went to the_____.
He read out the_____ from the
prophet_____. What he said was
good_____. But the people did not
like it. At first, they were_____. Then
they tried to_____ Jesus. But he
_____.

Isaiah	synagogue
news	kill
Nazareth	escaped
lesson	Sabbath
Galilee	surprised

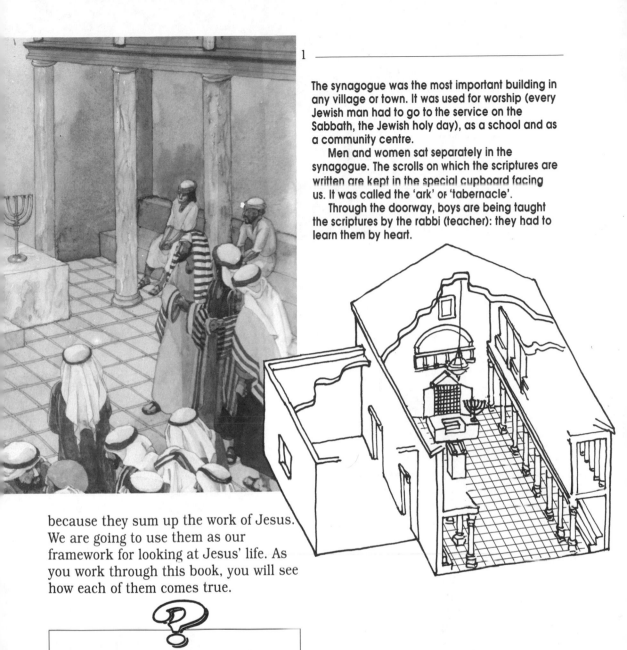

The synagogue was the most important building in any village or town. It was used for worship (every Jewish man had to go to the service on the Sabbath, the Jewish holy day), as a school and as a community centre.

Men and women sat separately in the synagogue. The scrolls on which the scriptures are written are kept in the special cupboard facing us. It was called the 'ark' or 'tabernacle'.

Through the doorway, boys are being taught the scriptures by the rabbi (teacher): they had to learn them by heart.

because they sum up the work of Jesus. We are going to use them as our framework for looking at Jesus' life. As you work through this book, you will see how each of them comes true.

● What does the word 'gospel' mean?

● Draw and label the diagram of the synagogue.

What Did Jesus Think About God?

The Jews believed in one God, who had made the universe. Long ago, he had rescued them when they were slaves in Egypt. He had given them Moses as their leader. Moses lived over 1200 years before Jesus. The Jews believed they were God's chosen people. God had given them the Law of Moses (the Torah) to live by, and the land of Israel as their home.

The Jews of Jesus' time thought of God as:

Jesus was a Jew, and he shared the beliefs of other Jews about God. But he took them much further, and added to them. For him, the most important thing is that God is Father:

● God is Father of the world
● God is Father of Jesus
● God is Father of Jesus' followers

CREATOR   GOOD   LAWGIVER

JUDGE   FATHER OF ISRAEL   KING OF HISTORY

Let's look at these ideas in turn.

GOD IS FATHER OF THE WORLD

Here are some things that Jesus said:

> 'Look at the birds flying around: they do not sow seeds, gather a harvest and put it in barns; yet your Father in heaven takes care of them.'

> 'It is God who clothes the wild grass—grass that is here today and gone tomorrow.'

God does not make the universe and then forget about it. His fatherly care is present all the time—he even cares about single blades of grass!

And God is not just Father of Israel. He is Father of the whole world, and of everybody in it.

> 'God makes the sun to shine on bad and good people alike, and gives rain to those who do good and to those who do evil.'

GOD IS FATHER OF JESUS

Jesus thought of God as his Father in a very special way. He would often go off on his own to pray. Mark's Gospel tells us a very surprising thing. Jesus called his Father 'Abba' when he prayed. 'Abba' is a Jewish word for 'Dad' or 'Daddy'. Children still use it today.

But there is something even more strange. Jesus says that he has been sent by his Father, and he calls himself 'the Son'. He even says,

> 'Whoever has seen me has seen the Father,'

and

> 'The Father and I are one.'

GOD IS FATHER OF JESUS' FOLLOWERS

God is the Father of Jesus in a very special way. But he is also the Father of Jesus' followers. Jesus wanted them to understand this. We can see it very clearly in this famous prayer he taught them. (Christians call this 'the Lord's Prayer' because Jesus himself gave it to them.)

> 'Our Father
> Who art in heaven
> Hallowed be thy name.
> Thy kingdom come,
> Thy will be done
> On earth as it is in heaven.
> Give us this day our daily bread
> And forgive us our trespasses
> As we forgive those who trespass against us
> And lead us not into temptation
> But deliver us from evil.'

(This is an old translation.)

> 'Our Father in heaven, may everybody honour you.
> Let your kingdom come, and what you want be done on earth, just as it is in heaven.
> Give us what we need to live today,
> and forgive us the things we have done wrong,
> just as we forgive the people who wrong us.
> Help us not to give in to evil things,
> and save us from them.'

(This is what the Lord's Prayer means.)

● Use what you have learnt from this chapter to write four short paragraphs. Begin each with one of these statements:

—The Jews thought that God was...

—Jesus taught that God was Father of the world when he said...

—Jesus showed that God was his Father when he said...

—Jesus taught that God was Father of his followers when he...

● Look up Matthew, chapter 6 in a Bible. Count up the number of times that Jesus called God 'Father'. What do you think this tells us about Jesus' view of God?

● You may know lots of Christians, or only a few. Ask one of them what she or he thinks it means to call God 'Father'. Share what you have found out with the rest of the class.

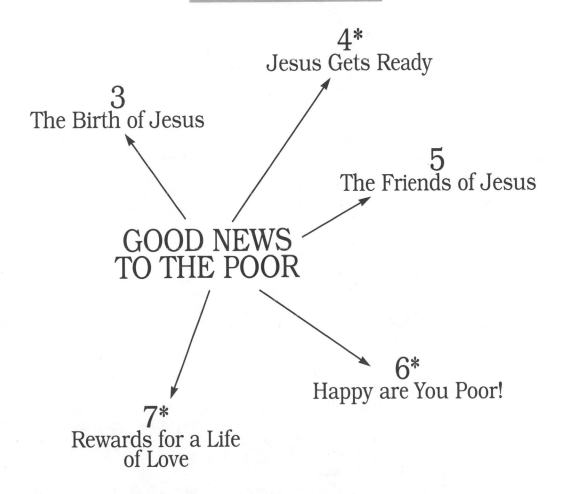

PART ONE

4*
Jesus Gets Ready

3
The Birth of Jesus

5
The Friends of Jesus

GOOD NEWS
TO THE POOR

6*
Happy are You Poor!

7*
Rewards for a Life
of Love

3

The Birth
of Jesus

The Gospels of Matthew and Luke tell us about Jesus' birth. Let's look at the story again. We tell you at the end of the paragraphs which bit is from Matthew, and which bit is from Luke.

● The angel Gabriel appeared to a priest called Zechariah in the Temple in Jerusalem. Gabriel said Zechariah's wife Elizabeth would have a son. When the boy grew up, he would get people ready for the Messiah. Zechariah could not believe it. Elizabeth was childless, and they were too old to have children. Because Zechariah did not believe that the angel was telling the truth, he was struck dumb until the promise came true. (Luke)

● Gabriel appeared to the virgin Mary. He told her she would also have a baby, God's promised king (Messiah). (Luke)

● Joseph—the man Mary had promised to marry—found out that Mary was pregnant. He had never slept with her, and decided to break off the engagement quietly. Before he could, an angel told him that the baby came from God. (Matthew)

● Mary was related to Elizabeth, and visited her. While she was there, Mary praised God with a long poem. (Luke)

● Elizabeth had her son, and he was called John. Zechariah could speak again, and he praised God. (Luke)

● The Romans were holding a census, and everyone had to go to his own town to be registered. Joseph took Mary to Bethlehem. (Luke)

● Jesus was born in Bethlehem. (Matthew and Luke)

● Mary wrapped Jesus in strips of cloth and laid him in a manger because there was no room at the inn. Shepherds visited them: angels had told them that the Messiah had been born. (Luke)

● Joseph and Mary took Jesus to the Temple in Jerusalem. This was to carry out Jewish religious ceremonies. An old man called Simeon, and an old woman called Anna, recognized Jesus as the Messiah and told others about him. (Luke)

● Wise men from the East arrived in Palestine. (Matthew never says there were three of them!) They had seen the new king's star, and wanted to find him. This upset Herod, the king of the Jews. Herod found out from the chief priests that the Messiah would be born in Bethlehem. He met the wise men, and sent them to discover exactly where the child was. They found Jesus in a house in Bethlehem, and gave him gold, frankincense and myrrh. God warned them in a dream not to go back to Herod. (Matthew)

● When they did not return, Herod flew into a rage. He ordered the deaths of all boys under two in the Bethlehem area, to make sure he killed this rival king. However, an angel warned Joseph, and the family escaped to Egypt. They stayed there until Herod was dead. (Matthew)

● The family went to live in Nazareth. (Luke and Matthew)

● Copy this table carefully:

Point No.	Matthew	Luke
1		Gabriel appears to Zechariah
2		
3		
4		
5		
6		
7		
8		
9		
10		
11		
12		
13		
14		

● Look at the fourteen points below. Place each one in the correct column. The first one has been done for you. Be careful: some go in both columns!

1 Gabriel appears to Zechariah
2 Gabriel appears to Mary
3 Angel appears to Joseph
4 Mary visits Elizabeth
5 Elizabeth gives birth
6 Census
7 Jesus born in Bethlehem
8 Jesus laid in a manger
9 Shepherds
10 Simeon and Anna
11 Wise men
12 Escape to Egypt
13 Murder of Bethlehem children
14 Family go to Nazareth

You will notice that Matthew's version is not the same as Luke's!

● The hero of Matthew's story is Joseph. We are told a lot about him. Who do you think is Luke's hero?

● The story most people know is a mixture of Matthew and Luke, plus some other details. These details were added later, and are not in the Bible. You may remember some from Christmas cards and Christmas carols.

List as many of these other details as you can think of. (Think about the wise men to get you started!) Read Matthew 1:18—2:23 and Luke 1:5—2:40 to help you.

THINGS TO NOTICE

● There are stories in the Old Testament about women becoming pregnant through a miracle. Like Elizabeth in Luke's Gospel, the women in those stories could not have children. Mary was able to have children, but she was a virgin. A virgin birth or conception may seem very strange. However, what it means is very important:

—Babies normally come from men

Mary, the mother-to-be of Jesus, greets her elderly relative Elizabeth, the mother-to-be of John. Their meeting was a high point, as each looked forward to the birth of a very special baby.

and women's love for each other. Christians say Jesus comes from God's love for the world.
—Christians believe Jesus is the Son of God: God became a man as Jesus.

So he could not have a human father.

● King Herod the Great ruled Israel for the Romans from 37BC until his death in 4BC. He was jealous, suspicious and cruel. He had hundreds of people murdered, including his wife and sons. He was quite capable of killing children in Bethlehem!

● Bethlehem was the home town of David, the greatest Jewish king. The Old Testament said the Messiah would be born there.

● **Christmas is about Jesus' birth.**

What things about the way people celebrate Christmas today do you think fit in well with this idea? What does not fit in so well, and why?

4*

Jesus Gets Ready

Only a few people knew about Jesus when he was growing up. But during all of that time the Jews were waiting for God to send them the Messiah. They thought that when he came they would enjoy a wonderful time of happiness. God himself would rule over them, and Israel would become the Kingdom of God.

The Jews did not know who the Messiah would be. But they thought they knew the sorts of things he would do. Long ago their prophets had looked into the future and had foreseen what would happen.

Some Jews even went out into the deserts of Israel to wait for the Messiah, because one of these prophets had said that his new age would begin in the wilderness. These Jews spent their time in prayer and study, and some of them gave up marriage and lived together rather like monks, devoting all their time to God. These were called Essenes.

Others wandered about on their own, praying for the coming of God's Kingdom and preaching. One of these was very important to Jesus: his cousin John. We have already come across him in the story of Jesus' birth. Now both he and Jesus are grown up.

When he became a man, John was given the nickname 'the Baptist', because he baptized people. Lots of religions have ceremonies when people are washed with water. For John it was a sign that the Jewish people were ready for the Messiah to arrive.

Jesus was baptized by John when he was about thirty. This is the first thing the Gospels tell us about Jesus' adult life. They make it clear that they think that Jesus' baptism was rather different from everybody else's. Jesus was not getting ready for the Messiah—he was the Messiah! Here is the version in

Matthew's Gospel (chapter 3, verses 13–17):

John the Baptist was given the task of preparing people for the coming of Jesus. He was a striking figure, preaching in the desert, and his words had the power to change lives.

'At that time Jesus arrived from Galilee and came to John at the River Jordan to be baptized by him. But John tried to make him change his mind. "I ought to be baptized by you," John said, "and yet you have come to me!"

'But Jesus answered him, "Let it be so for now. For in this way we shall do all that God requires." So John agreed.

'As soon as Jesus was baptized, he came up out of the water. Then heaven was opened to him, and he saw the Spirit of God coming down like a dove and alighting on him. Then a voice said from heaven, "This is my own dear Son, with whom I am pleased."'

The story of Jesus' baptism is meant to show us that Jesus was the Messiah. But what does that mean—what sort of Messiah would Jesus be?

Make a list of all the things you would do if somebody very special was coming to your home to talk to you. What similarities can you see between what you have written and what John the Baptist was doing? You might like to illustrate your answers with drawings.

One of the most common ideas people had about the Messiah in those days was that he would be a warrior king. He would be sent by God to lead the Jews in battle against the Romans and drive them out of Israel. This was a very popular idea among members of the Jewish resistance movement, the Zealots. They killed Roman soldiers when they could; they thought this was what God wanted.

Another idea was that the Messiah would be a sort of superman. He would have special powers so that he could do anything he wanted to. He would be protected from pain and suffering.

Would Jesus be anything like these?

The first three Gospels say that immediately after Jesus' baptism he went off alone into the desert and was

tempted by the Devil. Matthew and Luke give us the details. Look in the right-hand column to see what they mean.

Jesus has been going without food for forty days and nights. The Devil suggests to him that, since he is the Messiah, he has the power to turn the stones of the desert into bread for himself. Jesus refuses.	Jesus will refuse to use his powers as the Messiah for himself.
The Devil suggests to Jesus that he proves that he is the Son of God by throwing himself off the roof of the Temple in Jerusalem and emerging unharmed. Jesus refuses again.	Jesus is not going to be a superman type of Messiah.
The Devil points out that Jesus could rule the whole world if he wanted to. He shows Jesus all the kingdoms of the earth and offers them to him. Jesus refuses point-blank, and the Devil leaves him.	Jesus is not going to be a warrior king Messiah.

You can see that the story of Jesus' temptations is really about what sort of a Messiah Jesus will be. Every time the Devil says anything he suggests one of the popular ideas about what the Messiah should be like. But Jesus refuses them all.

Working in pairs, look up the story of Jesus' temptations in Matthew 4:1–11. Make up a play or short drama piece about it to practice and show to the rest of the class.

So Jesus' idea of what the Messiah should be like is not what people were expecting. Turn back to chapter 1 to see how Jesus thought of his work as the Messiah.

● John says that Jesus should really baptize him. Why do you think he says this?

● Religious people sometimes go without food out of obedience to God. Find out all you can about the Christian season of Lent and the idea of fasting.

5
The Friends of Jesus

Jesus needed a team to help him in his work. He had lots of followers, but he chose a small inner group. This group was given three names:

—the **apostles**, which means 'people who are sent' or 'ambassadors'
—the **disciples**, which means 'people who learn'
—or the **Twelve**. God's people, the Jews, were divided into *twelve* tribes. So Jesus chose *twelve* disciples. This showed they were the core of his new people, the Christians or the church. The Twelve (except Judas) went on to become the earliest Christians' leaders.

Other Jewish teachers had disciples, but they waited for their pupils to turn up. Jesus did not: he went to find people.

● When he was walking by Lake Galilee, Jesus called four fishermen: Simon and his brother Andrew, and James and his brother John. (Simon was also called Peter or Simon Peter.) 'Follow me,' Jesus told them, 'and I will teach you to catch men.' Their job would be to get others to join God's new people.

● These four were joined by a tax collector called Matthew, who worked nearby. People thought tax collectors were the scum of the earth. The money they collected went to the Roman government. They also took more than the Romans wanted, and kept the rest for themselves, so it is not surprising they were hated. When people saw Matthew and his friends eating with Jesus, they were outraged. 'Why does he eat with such people?' they demanded.

Jesus' reply is very important. It helps us understand how he saw his work:

> 'People who are well do not need a doctor, but only those who are sick. I have not come to call respectable people, but outcasts.'

Find the disciples' names in the wordsearch. Use Mark 3:16–19 to help you.

```
H P O L K B L L W X E D
A H E A M A T T H E W W
L I L T N N I I O D E B
P L A C E D V G A M I K
S I X D F R H Y O J C A
E P J A M E S L V U J P
T M O S T W O S C D A A
O F H E L H G I U A M M
X E N W T H O M A S E J
I T D R I L S O E R S I
W I A P O R S N N A Y W
I B E T H A D D A E U S
```

● Jesus' disciples were an odd bunch. They included the four fishermen, the tax collector, a Zealot revolutionary, and a traitor. They were not particularly good or religious. They were ordinary—even bad—people.

This idea has always been important for Christians, both long ago and today. Why do you think this is?

● Jesus' disciples left everything to follow him. Is there anything that would make you completely change your way of life?

● Look up the story of the fishermen in Mark 1:14–20 and Luke 5:1-11.
—What are the differences between Mark and Luke?
—Can you think of any reason or reasons to explain why the different writers say different things? (It may help you to know that Mark wrote before Luke.)

Share your ideas in a small group. If people come up with different reasons, try to work out which explanation is best.

about it. If their job were too easy, the disciples might become self-satisfied. They had to rely on God, especially as things were going to get tough. Jesus warned them, 'Everyone will hate you because of me.'

It is not surprising they did not want any of this at first. The Jews thought the Messiah would throw the Romans out of Palestine and then become Israel's king. At least some of the disciples wanted power and success. James and John asked Jesus for good jobs in his government. Peter could not bear the idea of Jesus dying for others. He thought that was not what a Messiah should do! But they had missed the point:

Jesus told them what being a disciple really meant:

'If anyone wants to come with me, he must forget self, carry his cross, and follow me.'

'Whoever wants to be first must place himself last and be the servant of all.'

Jesus told his disciples that they would be 'fishers of men'. To get their catch, they needed to spread the message about him. He said their job was
—to preach
—to teach
—to heal the sick.

So they behaved like Jesus, and carried on his work. He told them to travel light: they were not to use transport, carry lots of money or stay at the best hotels. They were not allowed to take any cash, food or even a clean shirt! This may all sound odd, but think

This means they must
—forget about power and what they want.
—care for and look after others (be their 'servants'). They must worry more about other people's needs than about their own.
—follow Jesus, even if it means they have to die for it ('carry their cross').

Eventually, they understood. Many of them died for their loyalty to Jesus. They were the servants of others, just as Jesus was the servant of everyone. For, as he said,

'Even the Son of Man did not come to be served; he came to serve and to give his life to redeem many people.'

(Jesus often called himself 'Son of Man'.)

Jesus said that self-interest and greed for power are 'out' for those who want to follow him; instead they must put other people's interests before their own and spend their lives in loving service.

● What does Jesus' idea of 'service' mean?

What do most people want from life? Is 'service' different? If so, how?
    You might want to discuss this in a small group and report back to the rest of the class.

● Read John 13:1–17, where Jesus washed the disciples' feet on the night before he died. What is he trying to show them? It is not as obvious as it looks!

6*

Happy are You Poor!

● Make a list of all the things you would most like for yourself. Now compare it with the list of the person sitting next to you. How many similarities are there—for instance, have you both chosen things to wear, or special sports equipment?

● Now have a go at estimating how much each list would cost. (You might need to ask your teacher to help you.) Is it a lot?

● How much would it cost to give everybody in the class exactly what he or she wanted?

Did any of you put down things that money cannot buy? What were they? Why did you include them?

Most of us want things—maybe fashion clothes, games, good food and somewhere pleasant to live. People were not very different in the time of Jesus, except that many of them thought that if they got everything they wanted it meant that God was pleased with them. They thought they were being rewarded for being good. Some of them seemed to think that if they were rich and successful, that was exactly what they deserved. They thought they were really splendid.

In Jesus' day, most of the rich were dead sure they would be the first ones in when God's Kingdom came.

WHAT DID JESUS THINK?
Jesus sometimes said some very surprising things. Sometimes he seems to turn all our normal ideas upside down. One of the most famous things he ever said was:

'Happy are you poor!
The Kingdom of heaven is yours!'

Jesus' teaching would have surprised the people of his time because he said that having lots of possessions was not a sign of being good after all. What mattered to God was how you lived your life, not how rich you were. The *really* wonderful people were those who did good even when they did not have very much themselves. And God's special people are not the rich, but the poor. God's Kingdom was especially for them.

The Gospels tell us that one day Jesus and his disciples were watching people putting money into the collection in the Temple in Jerusalem. Lots of rich men came along, very pleased with themselves because they were able to put in such large amounts. Then a poor widow put a tiny coin in, the smallest coin there was (for that reason this

Jesus watches a widow put two small coins into the offerings box outside the Temple. Because she gave all she had, it meant more in God's eyes than the costly gifts of the rich.

story is called 'the Widow's Mite'). Jesus said that the widow had really done much more than the rich men. They could easily afford what they gave away—but in her love, the widow had given all she had.

Jesus taught that the poor were specially close to God's heart: he cares for those at the bottom of the heap. His disciples were to serve the poor, even if this meant becoming poor themselves. Sometimes this caused trouble and lost him friends. One rich young man once asked Jesus what he had to do to be perfect. Jesus told him to sell everything he had and give the money away! But the young man couldn't bring himself to do it, and he went away sadly.

Look this story up for yourself in Matthew 19:16–22. Write a poem or a letter as though you were the rich man after his conversation with Jesus, expressing what you think he might have felt.

St Francis is an example from history of all the Christians who have devoted their whole lives to serving God, some giving up great wealth. Here St Francis is pictured 'preaching to the birds': one of many stories which tell of his special love for the animal kingdom and the whole of God's creation.

Although the rich young man went away, many followers of Jesus did give everything away. Peter and his brothers left everything and followed him, for instance. Down the centuries there have been some heroic examples of Christian service to the poor. You might like to do some projects in groups on some of these people, or any others you know about. (You might even have met some!)

Francis of Assisi gave up everything he had, and a very comfortable life, to live among the lepers of thirteenth-century Italy.

In our own day Mother Teresa of Calcutta has lived among the poorest of the poor in India for many years. She tries to care for the sick and dying.

How should Christians help the poor if they can't just give everything away—for instance, because they are at school or are married?

7*

Rewards for a Life of Love

Jesus asked a lot of his first followers. He said that they should be willing to give up their comfortable lives to follow him and to serve the poor. Being a disciple was not an easy business.

Imagine that you are one of Jesus' disciples. It is the end of a long day. You have spent nearly all of it helping Jesus with the crowds, walking from one place to another, listening and talking. Some people have been welcoming, but others have been hostile and rude. You are tired and hungry, and perhaps a bit fed up.

What thoughts might you now have about your new way of life? Discuss this with the person sitting next to you, and jot down one or two ideas. Here are some to start you off:

Jesus told stories to help people understand his teaching and his way of life. We call them **parables**.

One of the parables Jesus told would have helped the disciples when they were feeling fed up. It is called the Parable of the Sheep and the Goats, and it is in Matthew's Gospel (chapter 25, verses 31–46). It is about the Day of Judgment. That means the day when God will judge everybody after death. Most Jews believed in the Day of Judgment, and so did Jesus and his disciples. Christians today do as well. When Jesus talks about 'the Son of Man' or 'the King' in this story, he means himself.

> 'When the Son of Man comes as King and all the angels with him, he will sit on his royal throne, and the people of all the nations will be gathered before him. Then he will divide them into two groups, just as a shepherd separates the sheep from the goats. He will put the righteous people on his right and the others on his left. Then the King will say to the people on his right, "Come, you that are blessed by my Father! Come and possess the kingdom which has been prepared for you ever since the creation of the world. I was hungry and you fed me, thirsty and you gave me a drink; I was a stranger and you received me in your homes, naked and you clothed me; I was sick and you took care of me, in prison and you visited me."
>
> 'The righteous will then answer him, "When, Lord, did we ever see you hungry and feed you, or thirsty and give you a drink? When did we ever see you a stranger and welcome you in our homes, or naked and clothe you? When did we ever see you sick or in prison, and visit you?" The King will reply, "I tell you, whenever you did this for one of the least important of these brothers of mine, you did it for me!"'

In the story, Jesus says that when people care for anyone in need, they are really serving him! Even when they do not realize it, even when they are tired and discouraged, God sees their love. The disciples must not get fed up—they will be rewarded with everlasting happiness in heaven.

Jesus said, 'I was hungry and you fed me.' Christians today still find great inspiration in these words, and this is a group exercise to help you to tune in to what they feel.

Using Jesus' words as a title, make a poster or wall display for your classroom showing some of the work being done to help people who suffer today. You can use magazine articles and newspaper cuttings and their pictures.

So the followers of Jesus were offered heaven. Try to think for a moment of what that meant to them. Heaven is meant to be the best thing you can imagine or the most wonderful story you were ever told—only much, much better, and there for you to enjoy for ever.

We spend a lot of our time looking for things to make us happy. Jesus pointed out to his disciples that all the wealth in the world is fragile and unreliable. Moths could eat fine clothes, robbers could break in and steal—you could lose all your money overnight. Even today our nicest things get spoilt, and burglar alarms do not always work. Jesus told his disciples that they should look for the treasures that would last—the treasures of heaven. You can find some of these passages for yourselves in Matthew 6:19–21 and Luke 12:16–21 and 12:33–34.

SOME WARNINGS

But isn't this all a bit selfish still? Isn't there a danger that people will help the poor only to get themselves into heaven and to show other people how wonderfully religious they are?

Jesus knew people like that. He called them *hypocrites*, and he did not want his disciples to be like them. Instead, he said that they should help the poor with as little public display as possible. He once said that people who did things to show off to others got what they were looking for. They were after applause and a good reputation, and they got it. They had their reward already. But it was all pretty meaningless really,

Don't spend your lives piling up things that can be stolen, overnight, Jesus said. Much better concentrate on what pleases God, for no one can rob you of 'treasure in heaven'.

because praise from other people cannot last. What really matters is what God thinks of you, and he can see right into your heart. (Matthew 6:1–4)

People often say, 'His (or her) heart's in the right place,' when they are talking about someone else. What do they mean? Does your answer help you to understand the way Jesus said God saw people?

There were people in Jesus' time—no doubt there still are—who did nothing to help the poor. The Gospels have some very uncomfortable things to say about them—you can see the type of thing at the end of our Parable of the Sheep and the Goats (Matthew 25:41–46). People who close up their hearts to the poor are closing them to God, and so cannot get to heaven.

Here are some quick questions for you:

● In the story Jesus told, who are the sheep and the goats?

● What was, or is, the Day of Judgment?

● What was the reward Jesus said would be given to those who served him in the poor?

● What sort of person did Jesus say had already had their reward?

● What do we call the stories Jesus told?

● What were the treasures that Jesus said would last?

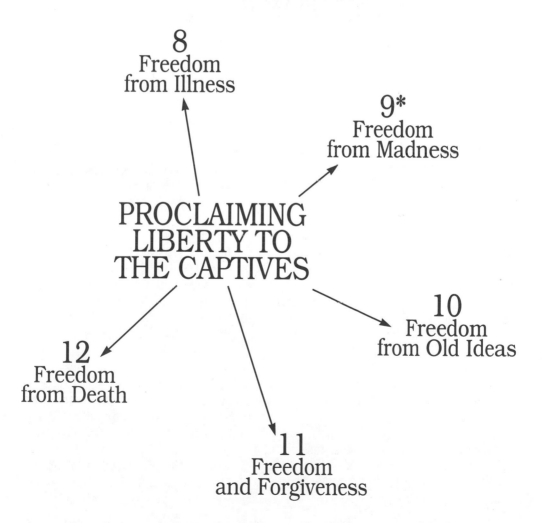

PART
TWO

8
Freedom
from Illness

9*
Freedom
from Madness

PROCLAIMING
LIBERTY TO
THE CAPTIVES

10
Freedom
from Old Ideas

12
Freedom
from Death

11
Freedom
and Forgiveness

8

Freedom from Illness

Jesus seems to have made the town of Capernaum his base for the early part of his work. Once, the house where he was staying got so full that the people spilled out on to the street. Why did they want to see him? Here are some possible reasons:

● they wanted to hear what he said.
● they wanted to find out whether he was the Messiah.
● they had heard strange rumours that he could do miracles.

These rumours seem to have reached four men in the town. They were bringing someone to see Jesus. He was paralysed, so they had to carry him. We take up the story from Mark's Gospel, chapter 2:

'Because of the crowd, however, they could not get the man to him. So they made a hole in the roof right above the place where Jesus was. When they had made an opening, they let the man down, lying on his mat. Seeing how much faith they had, Jesus said to the paralysed man, "My son, your sins are forgiven."'

It is easy to see that the men had faith (or trust) in Jesus, but what he says seems odd. Someone is ill, and Jesus tells him that his sins arc forgiven!

We can explain it like this:

● Jewish people in Jesus' time thought sin (doing or thinking evil) could actually make you ill. One teacher or rabbi said, 'If you are ill, you will not get better until all your sins are forgiven.'

● Perhaps the paralysed man thought like this. He was frightened because he thought God was angry with him.

Houses in Palestine in Jesus' time had flat roofs, which you reached by an outside staircase. The roofs were made from wooden beams about a metre apart. The space between them was filled with clay and twigs. It would have been easy to make a hole in this, although very annoying for the owner!

● Jesus wanted him to know that it was all right. God was not angry. The man was not being punished: his sins were forgiven.

Why do you think people thought sin caused illness? Do you agree with them?

What Jesus said got the paralysed man into trouble with some people called the **Pharisees.**

The Pharisees were very religious men. They wanted to keep God's Law and to help other people to keep it. The Law, or **Torah**, was the heart of the Jewish faith. It still is today. The Jews believed that God gave the Torah to Moses. Moses was the great Jewish leader when God's people were slaves in Egypt. He led them out to freedom in about 1250BC.

Like all Jews, the Pharisees believed the Torah showed them how to live. They did not want to break its rules, even by accident. So they added extra

The Torah is the first five books in the Jewish Bible or Tenakh, the Christian Old Testament.

Look up the names of the books in a Bible. Copy and complete this 'Torah bookshelf'.

rules, and learned them by heart. For example, the Torah said people must have one day a week for rest and worship. This day was called the Sabbath, and no one should have to work. But what did 'work' mean? Did it just mean people should have a day off, or was it more? The Pharisees said that it meant more than not doing a job. They said it meant you could not walk more than a kilometre, and could not even write a letter. Rules like this got harder and harder to keep. Some Pharisees looked down on people who could not or did not keep them.

When Jesus told the paralysed man that his sins were forgiven, some

The friends of the man on the stretcher are sure that Jesus can heal him, but they cannot push through the crowds—so they carry him up to the roof, and break through! This is a story with a happy ending.

Pharisees said to themselves, 'How does he dare to talk like this? This is blasphemy. God is the only one who can forgive sins!' ('Blasphemy' means 'insulting God'.)

Jesus asked them, 'Is it easier to say to this paralysed man, "Your sins are forgiven," or to say, "Get up, pick up your mat, and walk"? I will prove to you, then, that the Son of Man has authority on earth to forgive sins.'

He turned to the man, and told him to pick up his mat and go home. Mark's Gospel finishes the story by saying, 'While they all watched, the man got up, picked up his mat, and hurried away. They were all completely amazed and praised God, saying, "We have never seen anything like this!"'

In this story, Jesus heals a man and forgives his sins. We could say this means he is *completely* cured. There are many other stories of Jesus' miracles. They are not about magic or conjuring tricks. There are no 'magic words' or mumbo-jumbo. They affect human beings. They show that God is powerful and cares about people. And they show that what Jesus does is what God does.

Write a short paragraph about the Pharisees, in your own words.

Freedom
from Madness

Imagine that you are dreaming. You find yourself in the middle of a crowd. A crowd of angry and dangerous people, looking for trouble. You do not want to be there, but you would draw attention to yourself if you tried to get away.

Suddenly, a riot breaks out. There is chaos and confusion. The mob turns on you. You see their vicious faces looming up. You are convinced that you will be attacked. Then, to your terror and astonishment, you realize it is far worse. *You are absorbing the crowd.* You can still sense their rage and hatred, but they are now inside your mind. They are so real that you know this is not a dream. This is really happening. You look around in panic for the mob, and cannot see it. But it is still there. It has become part of you. And when you realize it, you go mad.

The Gospels say that Jesus met a man who was convinced something like this had happened to him. This madman would shriek like a wild animal, and gash himself with sharp stones. He had become a danger to himself and others. The people from his town could not control him. They had tried chaining him up, but he was so strong that he simply broke the chains. It is not surprising that they were frightened of him. Mark and Luke say he called himself 'Legion'. Some English Bibles translate this as 'Mob'. A *legion* was a large number of men in the Roman army: they were often a disorderly *mob*. The man believed that he was possessed —by a mob of demons.

Legion took to living among the tombs by Lake Galilee. Jesus and his disciples arrived there by boat. As soon as he saw them, Legion ran to meet them.

'Jesus, Son of the Most High God!' he bellowed. 'What do you want with me?' Somehow he knew who Jesus was. Jesus did not answer his question. This is what Luke says happened next (chapter 8, verses 26–39):

> 'There was a large herd of pigs nearby, feeding on a hillside. So the demons begged Jesus to let them go into the pigs, and he let them. They went out of the man and into the pigs. The whole herd rushed down the side of the cliff into the lake and was drowned.'

Legion was cured. The people looking after the pigs ran off, and spread the news in the town. When the locals heard that the lunatic was now perfectly sane, they were amazed. It was too much to take, so they asked Jesus to leave. Legion wanted to go with him, but Jesus told him, 'Go back home to your family and tell them how much the Lord has done for you and how kind he has been to you.'

He went through the whole area, telling people what had happened to him.

Parts of this story may seem rather strange to us. Some people find it hard to believe that Jesus ordered a mob of evil spirits to go into a herd of pigs. They say the pigs ran off because Legion had a fit which frightened them. Or they say a story about a madman has become mixed up with a story about some pigs drowning. But people in Jesus' time did believe in demons. Here are some of the ideas they had about them:

● Demons wanted to hurt human beings. They could make you ill, or even mad.

● They usually lived outdoors: in woods, gardens or vineyards, and among tombs.

● They were particularly dangerous at night, and in the midday heat.

● There were over seven million of them. You would die from shock if you realized how many demons surrounded you.

Across Lake Galilee, Jesus and his friends come upon a madman who has everyone terrified. The man calls himself 'Legion' (or 'Mob') because he believes he is possessed by violent demons.

Why do you think people in Jesus' time believed in demons? Do you think they were right?

called psychiatrists or psychotherapists. Legion may have had a rare, and violent, form of mental illness.

Today, most of us would probably say Legion was mentally ill. Mental illness is simply any disease which affects the mind. We all get sad, depressed, angry or frightened at times. It does not usually last long. Mentally ill people have feelings like these, but they are very extreme and can last for months or even years. They can be treated by drugs, or by special doctors

What do you think? Was Legion mentally ill, or possessed by demons? Does it make any difference? Remember to give your reasons.

So the Gospels show Jesus healing people from madness as well as illness. He allows them to become whole, and sets them free.

● The sentences below tell the story of the madman in the tombs. However, they have got jumbled up. Write them out in the correct order.

    —The pigs drowned.

    —Jesus and the disciples arrived on the shore of Lake Galilee.

    —The people from the town asked Jesus to leave.

    —The demons went into the pigs, and they ran off a cliff.

    —A madman called Legion ran to meet Jesus.

    —Legion wanted to go with Jesus, but Jesus told him to go home to his family.

    —The demons asked Jesus to send them into some pigs which were feeding nearby.

● The miracle stories of Jesus casting out demons are called *exorcisms*. Try to look up these stories of exorcisms in the Gospels:

    —Luke 4:31—37

    —Matthew 12:22—32

    —Mark 9:14—29

10
Freedom from Old Ideas

Can you remember being told any good stories when you were younger? Perhaps your parents told them to you, or you heard them first at school. What were they?

Jot down their names. Do you think these would have been different if you had been brought up in a country far away? Why?

Perhaps you or your parents come from another country, and you have noticed that your stories are rather different from those of your classmates. You might like to share one of them by telling it to the rest of the class.

The stories we are told as small children often stay with us for the rest of our lives. It is quite likely that when we are older we will find ourselves telling them to our own children! In this way traditions grow up.

Parents sometimes tell their children stories because they hope that the stories will have a good influence on them. What things influence us when we are older? Here are some ideas:

All of us are influenced by traditions of one sort or another. These traditions are often full of beauty and wisdom. They help us to feel secure and to make some sense of the world.

Sometimes, however, traditions can clash. Different people have different ideas about how the world should be. Instead of learning to live together, they begin to hate each other. Sometimes hatred of another group of people can even become part of the tradition we learn.

Something like this was going on at the time of Jesus. There was a lot of hatred between the Jews and the **Samaritans**.

The Samaritans lived in the area shown shaded on the map. This had

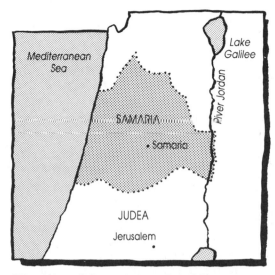

This modern photograph shows Palestinian women carrying water from a well. It helps us picture the scene of Jesus' discussion with the woman from Samaria.

once belonged to the Israelites, but in 721BC that part of Israel had been conquered by the Assyrians, a great power of that time. The Assyrians were very cruel. They forced many of the Israelites to leave their homes and work as slaves. They took over their farms and houses and gave them to Assyrians, who settled in Samaria and had children. In this way the Assyrian settlers and the Israelites who remained eventually became one people, the Samaritans.

By the time of Jesus, the Assyrian Empire had long since vanished. Samaria was ruled by the Romans, just like Judea and Galilee, where the Jews lived (look at the map). But over the years the Jews and the Samaritans had drifted apart.

Somehow the religion of the Samaritans had survived, but it had become very different from the Jewish way of doing things. For instance, the Samaritans said that the most important place for worshipping God was on a mountain in Samaria called Mount Gerizim, while the Jews said it was the Temple in Jerusalem. So, although they shared some beliefs, they belonged to different traditions— traditions which encouraged hatred between the two groups. The Gospels tell us that 'the Jews had nothing to do with the Samaritans'.

But Jesus did! John's Gospel (chapter 4) tells a story about a meeting between Jesus and a Samaritan woman.

Jesus was travelling between Judea and Galilee. Look at the map—you can see that this meant he had to cross Samaria or go a very long way round. He was tired and hot, because it was midday and the sun was at its fiercest.

Jesus sat down by a well to rest, outside a Samaritan town called Sychar. Soon a woman came to draw some water. (There were no pipes or taps in Palestine in those days: you had to fetch and carry all the water you needed, as you still do in many developing countries today.)

At this point, an ordinary Jewish man would have got up and walked away. Jewish tradition said that you should steer clear of Samaritans, and especially Samaritan women. But Jesus does not seem to care about that. Instead, he asks the woman for a drink. Not surprisingly, she is astonished.

'What?' she says. 'You are a Jew— and you are asking me for a drink?'

Jesus and the woman start talking. The woman begins to realize that there is something special about Jesus, so she asks him—where should people really worship God? On Mount Gerizim, or in Jerusalem? But Jesus' answer is to say that all of that stuff is in the past. God is doing a new thing. The true worshippers of God are now those who worship him 'in Spirit and in truth', in their hearts.

What are we to make of this story? Here are two ideas:

● Old ways of thinking can trap us into hating people and stop us from caring about them. The Jews and the Samaritans had traditions which did this.

● Jesus says that God wants a *new way of thinking*. People who welcome what he is doing have to be willing to give up old hatreds.

In groups, think about the meaning of the story. Can you think of anywhere the story might be particularly useful today? Why?

Make a report and read it to the rest of the class.

We will be hearing more about Samaritans later on in this book. You could help your learning now by drawing up a 'Basic Facts File' about them using the information in this chapter. We have made the first entry for you to copy below: try to add some more to it.

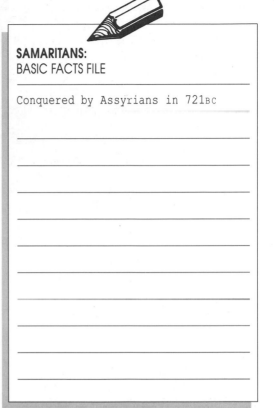

SAMARITANS:
BASIC FACTS FILE

Conquered by Assyrians in 721BC

Freedom and Forgiveness

What we say, or what we do, can cause pain. If we are honest, we will admit that. Sometimes we want things to hurt, sometimes not. If someone hurts us, what can we do?

● Never speak to them again?
● Say it doesn't matter, but want to get our own back?
● Be polite to them, but never trust thcm again or havc them as a friend?
● Forgive them?

Think these options through carefully. None of them is very easy. In the long run, which do you think is best?

When Jesus talked about forgiveness, he did not mean simply letting people off. It is not this:

It is certainly not like this:

Forgiveness rules out revenge. It also works two ways. It is much more like this:

Jesus told people they must forgive others. This means that they must be *ready* and *willing* to forgive. But forgiveness has to be accepted as well as given. (Just as if I want to give you some money, you have to take it!) Accepting forgiveness would mean being sorry, and ready to 'repair the damage' if need be. So,

Forgiveness = giving + accepting
(being ready (being sorry,
to forgive) and ready
to make
amends).

Write two short paragraphs to explain this.

● Begin one, 'Forgiveness is...'
● Begin the other, 'Forgiveness is not...'

You could design your own cartoons instead.

In the Lord's Prayer (which we talked about in chapter 2), Jesus taught the disciples to pray,

'Forgive us our sins,
as we forgive those who sin against us.'

There are several stories in the Gospels which show how to do this. This chapter looks at two of them. One is a story Jesus told. The other is a story about him.

THE WOMAN CAUGHT IN ADULTERY
This story is recorded in John's Gospel, chapter 8.

Jesus was teaching in the Temple in Jerusalem. While he was there, the Pharisees and the scribes (experts in the Jewish Law) brought a woman before him. She had been caught committing adultery. This broke one of the Ten Commandments in the Torah. The Torah said that the penalty for adultery was death. The Jewish method of execution was stoning. The men asked Jesus what he thought they should do.

They were trying to trap him. If he said, 'It doesn't matter,' people would stop following him. No good Jewish teacher— let alone the Messiah—would go against the Law. If he said, 'Stone her,' they could get the Romans to arrest him. The Romans did not allow the Jews to execute anyone. (If the scribes and Pharisees were going to stone her, which seems likely, it would be illegal. It would be a lynching, a mob murder.) While they waited for their answer, Jesus calmly wrote on the ground with his finger. Then he looked up.

'Whichever one of you has committed no sin,' he said, 'may throw the first stone at her.' He bent down again and continued writing. His words sank home.

There were many synagogues, but only one Temple. The first Temple was built by the great King Solomon, nearly 1,000 years before Jesus. It was destroyed in 587BC by an invading army from Babylonia, but it was rebuilt. Herod the Great added to the buildings.

The Jews believed that only in the Temple could animal sacrifices be offered to God, and that God had ordered it to be built. It was the most holy place in the world.

The Temple was finally destroyed in AD70 by the Romans. Even today, Jews remember this with sadness.

Gradually, they all left, leaving just Jesus and the woman.

'Where are they?' he asked her. 'Is there no one left to condemn you?'

'No one, sir,' she answered.

'Well, then,' Jesus said, 'I do not condemn you either. Go, but do not sin again.'

Notice:

● Jesus' reply is brilliant. It avoids the trap, *and* makes them think.

● Jesus does not say what the woman has done is all right. It is wrong, but she is still a person God cares about, like everybody else. Forgiveness means hating the sin, but loving the sinner.

THE PRODIGAL SON

'Prodigal' means 'wasteful'. 'The Prodigal Son' is the name given to one of the parables Jesus told. (You can find it in Luke, chapter 15.) The story goes like this:

There was a rich man who had two sons. In his will, he had divided what he owned between them. One day, his younger son said to him, 'Give me my share of the property now.' The father gave it to him,

and the young man went abroad. He lived recklessly, and wasted the lot. When it was gone, he was penniless. Worse still, a famine hit the country. He took a job as a farm labourer, looking after pigs. By now, he was so hungry that even the pig food looked good. Then he came to his senses. 'All my father's hired workers have more than they can eat, and here I am about to starve!' he thought. 'I will get up and go to my father and say, "Father, I have sinned against God and against you. I am no longer fit to be called your son; treat me as one of your hired workers."'

He was still some way from home when his father saw him and ran to meet him. He was not interested in his son's idea. He was so pleased to see him that he decided to throw a party.

The elder boy came home to find the feast going on. When he found out it was for his brother, he was so angry that he would not even go into the house. 'All these years I have worked for you like a slave,' he complained to his father outside. 'I have never disobeyed your orders. But this son of yours wasted all your property, and when he comes back, you

Jesus' story of the 'prodigal son', tells of a man who wasted all his money. At last, so hungry he would gladly have eaten the husks he fed to the pigs, he decided to go home and throw himself on his father's mercy. It is a 'parable' story with a deeper meaning about God's love.

kill the prize calf for him!'

'My son,' the father replied, 'you are always here with me, and everything I have is yours. But we had to celebrate and be happy, because your brother was dead, but now he is alive; he was lost, but now he has been found.'

Pick one of the two stories about forgiveness.

● **Briefly tell the story in your own words.**

● **Explain what you think it is saying**
—**about forgiveness**
—**about God.**

● **If you have time, draw and label the diagram of the Temple.**

12

Freedom from Death

All of us come across death from time to time, and it is usually upsetting. Members of our family and people we love die, and one day so shall we. Death can make us feel angry, afraid and lonely.

Death was a problem for the Jews of Jesus' time as well. In fact, things were even more difficult for them. They had very few medicines, and there were many diseases. Childhood was particularly dangerous. Many parents had to watch helplessly while their children died from diseases we can cure very easily today.

> RELIGION IS JUST A CUSHION FOR PEOPLE WHO CAN'T FACE UP TO DEATH.

Have you ever heard people say something like that? But history teaches us that this is not true. Long before Jesus came, the ancient Jews believed in God—but they did not believe in life after death! They seem to have thought that life just stopped when you died, and yet they went on saying their prayers.

Some Jews—the **Sadducees**—still thought like this at the time of Jesus. The Sadducees were mainly from the most important families in Jerusalem, where their men were priests in the Temple.

However, most Jews were not Sadducees, and by Jesus' time they had come to believe that there would be a life after death. They looked forward to what they called the 'resurrection of the dead'. This was supposed to happen on a day right at the end of time. God would raise all the dead, and they would

Lazarus' tomb was a cave in the rock with a stone rolled over its entrance. This was a common way of burying bodies in Palestine in New Testament times, especially in the hill-country, where there was little soil.

then be judged according to how much good or bad they had done in their lives. (This is also called the Day of Judgment. We came across it earlier, when we were looking at the Parable of the Sheep and the Goats in chapter 7.)

If you think about it, the resurrection of the dead is quite a sensible idea. If God exists, it seems unlikely that he would create people and then snuff them out like candles after seventy years or so.

So Jesus and his followers belong to the majority group who believed in life after death. But the Gospels take things much further than that. Several stories about Jesus actually talk about him raising people from the dead. The most famous is called *The Raising of Lazarus*. This is the story, from John 11:1–44:

Jesus had three friends. They were Martha and Mary, who were sisters, and their brother Lazarus. They lived in a village called Bethany, not far from Jerusalem.

One day, when Jesus was preaching many miles away, Lazarus became very ill. His sisters knew Jesus could heal the sick, and so they sent a message asking him to come.

Jesus set off, but before he reached him, Lazarus died. By the time Jesus got near to Bethany, Lazarus' body had been in its tomb for four days. Martha and Mary were beside themselves with grief. When Jesus came near, Martha ran out to meet him.

'Lord,' she said through her tears, 'if only you had got here earlier, my brother would not have died!'

Jesus looked at her. 'Your brother will rise again,' he said.

'I know that,' sobbed Martha. 'I know he will rise again at the resurrection on the last day.' But that was not what Jesus meant. He looked at her and said, 'I am the resurrection and the life. Whoever believes in me will live, even though he dies; and whoever lives and believes in me will never die. Do you believe this?'

'Yes,' said Martha. 'I do believe that you are the Messiah, the Son of God, who was to come into the world.'

Martha ran to fetch Mary, who was still in the house, and they took Jesus to Lazarus' tomb. Martha and Mary were still weeping, and so were all the other mourners. Jesus felt so sorry for them that he cried too.

Standing outside the tomb, Jesus told them to roll away the stone from its entrance. At first Martha protested—there would be a terrible smell—but then it was done. Jesus raised his eyes and prayed to God his Father, then shouted out loud: 'Lazarus! Come out!'

Lazarus came out of the tomb, still wrapped in his grave-clothes, but alive and well. 'Unbind him,' said Jesus, 'and let him go.'

The Gospel writers chose their stories very carefully. They are often packed with hidden meanings. In the raising of Lazarus, the hidden meaning is that Jesus brings freedom from death. Look at the story again. Martha says she knows that Lazarus will rise again on the last day. But that must have seemed a very long way off to her then. It was not much comfort! By raising Lazarus from the dead Jesus showed her (and everybody else) that hope and freedom in the face of death is much nearer than she had thought. To know Jesus is to know God in action—and God brings things to life and raises the dead. That is why Jesus says, 'I am the resurrection and the life.'

This is a very important idea. We will be looking at it again towards the end of this book.

● Where did Martha and Mary live?

● Why didn't Martha want the stone rolled away from Lazarus' tomb?

● Why had Martha and Mary sent a messenger to Jesus?

● What did the Sadducees think about life after death, and how was this different from what other Jews believed?

● Christian funerals often begin by somebody quoting some words of Jesus which appear in this chapter. Can you guess which ones they are? Why do you think they are appropriate?

Here are some more stories for you to read. You will need to look them up in your Bible:

● Jesus raises a widow's dead son: Luke 7:11–17.

● The Sadducees try to make fun of Jesus because of what he says about life after death: Mark 12:18–27.

● Another story about Martha and Mary: Luke 10:38–42.

PART THREE

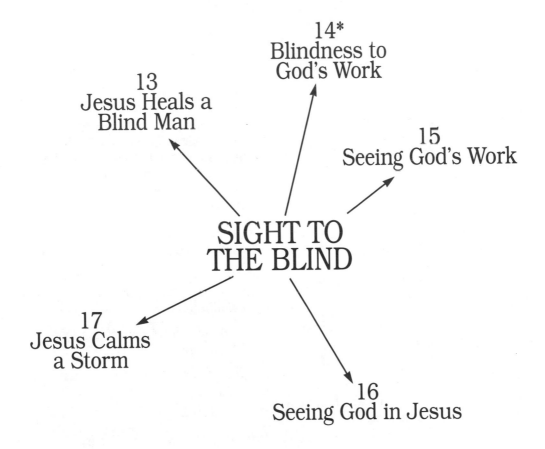

13
Jesus Heals a
Blind Man

14*
Blindness to
God's Work

15
Seeing God's Work

SIGHT TO THE BLIND

17
Jesus Calms
a Storm

16
Seeing God in Jesus

13
Jesus Heals a Blind Man

The play script which follows is based on a story in John's Gospel (chapter 9).

Characters:

Narrator	Man
Jesus	Pharisee 1
Disciple (Peter)	Pharisee 2
Neighbour 1	Mother
Neighbour 2	Father

Narrator: One Sabbath in Jerusalem, Jesus and his disciples came across a blind man. He made his living by begging. One of the disciples asked Jesus a question.

Peter: Teacher, whose sin made him be born blind? Was it his own, or his parents'?

Jesus: His blindness has nothing to do with his sins or his parents' sins.

Narrator: The disciples were surprised. Like most Jews of their time, they thought sin caused illness. Jesus bent down, and made a paste on the ground from spit and mud. He put this on the blind man's eyes.

Jesus: Go to the Pool of Siloam, and wash your face.

Narrator: When he did, he found he could see. He was amazed, and so were his neighbours.

Neighbour 1: That's not the man who used to sit and beg, is it?

Neighbour 2: No, it can't be. It just looks a bit like him, that's all.

Neighbour 1: It is you, isn't it?

Man: Yes. That man Jesus cured me.

Neighbour 2: Jesus? Well, where's he got to, then?

Man: I don't know.

Neighbour 1: I think we'd better take this fellow to the Pharisees.

Narrator: Later...

Pharisee 1: You said you were blind, didn't you? How did you get your sight back, then?

Man: (getting rather fed up with saying it again): Jesus put some mud on my eyes. I washed my face, and then I could see.

Pharisee 1: I don't like this. Nobody who was really from God would heal people today. God himself says we must not work on the Sabbath. It's in the Torah!

Pharisee 2: But surely a bad man couldn't do miracles?

Narrator: There was an argument.

Pharisee 1: You're telling us this man cured your blindness. What have you

The Gospels tell of several times when Jesus cured blind people. The most famous is in John's Gospel where it provides a vivid demonstration of Jesus' claim to be 'the light of the world'.

got to say about him?

Man: He's a prophet.

Pharisee 2: Why don't we get his parents in? They might know something.

Narrator: The Pharisees found them, and the investigation continued.

Pharisee 2: You say your son was born blind. How can he see now?

Mother: I don't know. I don't know who cured him, either.

Father: Why don't you ask him? He's old enough to speak for himself.

Narrator: When the Pharisees realized the parents could not help them, they called the son back.

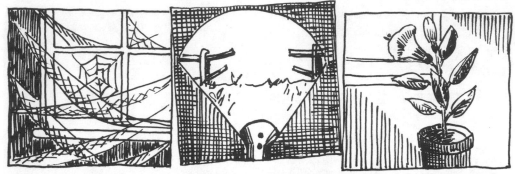

Pharisee 1: I order you by God to tell the truth. That man whom you say cured you is a sinner. What happened?

Man: I don't know whether he's a sinner or not. What I do know is that I was blind, and now I can see.

Pharisee 2: What did he do to you? *How* did he cure you?

Man: How many more times do I have to tell you? Why don't you listen? Why do you want to hear it again, anyway? Do you want to become his disciples as well?

Pharisee 1: How dare you say that? Who do you think we are?

Pharisee 2: *You're* that fellow's disciple, not us. We are Moses' disciples. We know that God spoke to Moses. As for that man, we don't even know where he came from!

Man: This is stupid. Jesus healed my blindness, and you can't work out where he comes from! Nobody's ever done anything like this before. God doesn't listen to sinners. He only listens to people who respect him and do what he wants. If Jesus wasn't from God, he could never have done it.

Pharisee 1: You were born and brought up a sinner. Who are you to teach us? Get out: you're banned from the synagogues.

Light shows up the things we need to clear away; it alerts us to the dangers of the dark; it is essential for life and growth. The candle often given at baptism reminds believers of Jesus as 'the light of the world'.

Narrator: When Jesus heard what had happened, he went to find the man. He had a question to ask him.

Jesus: Do you believe in the Son of Man?

Man: Tell me who he is, sir. Then I'll believe in him!

Jesus: You have already seen him. You are speaking to him now.

Man: Lord, I believe.

In this story:

● Do you think the man is the same sort of person after he is cured? If not, what is the difference?

● Why do you think the cure worried the Pharisees so much?

Right at the beginning of this story, Jesus said this:

'I am the light of the world.'

In some ways, this is the key to the miracle. Many of us were afraid of the dark when we were children. Being left in a dark room was very frightening. Think of the relief when the light went on! Life in the world, too, can be dark and mysterious. Is this all there is? Is it worth bothering with? Is there a God? What happens when we die?

John's Gospel says Jesus called himself the *light of the world*. This means:

● He is the light that brings certainty into the darkness of the world.

● The blind man comes into light from darkness when he meets Jesus. Any encounter with Jesus means coming from darkness into light.

There are other stories in the Gospels where Jesus gives sight to the blind. Read them in

—Mark 10:46—52
—Matthew 20:29—34
—Mark 8:22—26

14*

Blindness to God's Work

In the last chapter, we saw how Jesus healed the man born blind. When the meeting with the Pharisees was over, the man realized who Jesus was. Jesus then said,

> 'I came to this world to judge, so that the blind should see and those who see should become blind.'

We have seen how Jesus brought sight to the blind.

'I see' can sometimes mean 'I understand'. There are always some people who will ignore what is staring them in the face. They are the sort of people who say, 'I've made up my mind, don't confuse me with the facts.' They think they 'see'. They are wrong, but they are quite sure they are right. Jesus means that he will show these people in

their true colours. They cannot 'see'; they are 'blind'.

When he said this, the Pharisees asked, 'Surely you don't mean that we are blind, too?' Jesus' reply is very important:

> 'If you were blind, you would not be guilty. You are guilty because you are convinced that you can see.'

In other words:

If they *really* could not understand, the Pharisees would not be guilty.

They are guilty because they have convinced themselves that they are right. Deep down, they know they are wrong. But they refuse to admit it.

The Gospels show the Pharisees often getting things badly wrong. They are blind to what God really wants, and to what God is doing in Jesus.

Once, they saw him and his disciples picking some corn in a field. In those days, this was not stealing. Farmers allowed travellers to eat some of the corn as they went past. The Pharisees did not like it because that day was a Sabbath. God said in the Torah that people should rest and worship on the Sabbath. Work was forbidden—and the Pharisees counted rubbing the ears of corn between your hands as work. When the Pharisees challenged Jesus about it, he said:

> 'The Sabbath was made for the good of man; man was not made for the Sabbath.'

In other words, people and their needs are more important than rules, even the rules of the Torah. He annoyed them even more when he added:

> 'The Son of Man is Lord even of the Sabbath.'

Jesus meant he had the authority to change things. The old ways, which the Pharisees liked, were not so important now. They would have been very shocked by what he said. It went against all their ideas about God.

Not all the Pharisees were like the ones in the Gospels. Many—perhaps most—were good men who really tried to help other people and to do what God wanted.

Let's look at something else Jesus taught about the Pharisees.

THE PARABLE OF THE PHARISEE AND THE TAX COLLECTOR

This parable comes from Luke's Gospel, chapter 18. (When you read it, remember that people in Jesus' time hated tax collectors. They worked for the Romans and were often very greedy.)

'Once there were two men who went up to the Temple to pray: one was a Pharisee, the other a tax collector.

'The Pharisee stood apart by himself and prayed, "I thank you, God, that I am not greedy, dishonest, or an adulterer, like everybody else. I thank you that I am not like that tax collector over there. I fast two days a week, and I give you a tenth of all my income."

'But the tax collector stood at a distance and would not even raise his face to heaven, but beat on his breast and said, "God, have pity on me, a sinner!."

'"I tell you," said Jesus, "the tax collector, and not the Pharisee, was in the right with God when he went home. For everyone who makes himself great will be humbled, and everyone who humbles himself will be made great."'

● Read the last paragraph of the parable again.

—The tax collector is in the right with God when he goes home, not the Pharisee. Why?

—Jesus said, 'Everyone who makes himself great will be humbled, and everyone who humbles himself will be made great.' What do you think he means?

● The people who first heard this parable were the Jews of Jesus' day. Think about what it says, and what you know about tax collectors, then:

—How do you think Jesus' audience reacted to the story?

—The parable is still important to Christians, nearly two thousand years later. What is it about the story which makes it so effective?

● Write a paragraph to explain what Jesus taught about the Pharisees.

● Draw a comic strip of the Parable of the Pharisee and the Tax Collector. (You will find it easier to do a rough design first!)

Seeing God's Work

Do you spend much time reading or watching television?

Who are the 'baddies' in the stories? Make a list with the person sitting next to you.

'Baddies' are good fun in fiction. They make books and films exciting.

There are even some traditional ones.

Real life is usually more complicated than stories. Even so, you can probably think of times when you have felt lonely, or when people seemed to be against you.

It was the same in Jesus' time. Some

people were disliked. Remember that tax collectors were hated because they worked for the Romans and often were dishonest and greedy.

Luke's Gospel (chapter 19) tells a story about Jesus and a tax collector called Zacchaeus. Although he was rich and lived in a big house in Jericho, nobody liked him much. The religious people called him a sinner—and he was very short!

One day, Jesus was passing through Jericho with his disciples. He was well known by now, and crowds of people came to see him wherever he went.

Zacchaeus wanted to see Jesus. He ran into the crowd, but there were so many people, and they were so much taller than he was, that he could see nothing. So he decided to run on ahead. He climbed a sycamore fig-tree and looked out at Jesus through the branches.

Jesus saw him. 'Zacchaeus,' he said, 'hurry up and come down. I must stay In your house today.' Everybody was shocked and astonished. Jesus was meant to be a holy man, yet he was going into the house of a sinner. But the effect on Zacchaeus was the most startling thing of all. He welcomed Jesus gladly. He promised to give away to the poor half of everything he owned. He even said that if he had taken money from people dishonestly, he would pay them back four times as much.

Jesus was pleased. 'Salvation has come to this house today!' he said. 'The Son of Man came to seek and save the lost.'

Jesus' kindness changed Zacchaeus. Although he had done some pretty terrible things, he was big enough to recognize them and to make amends. He is an example of someone who was

● How do you think Zacchaeus felt about the way people treated him before he met Jesus?

● Jesus showed Zacchaeus kindness. Why might this have changed him?

● Christians would say that this story has an important message about the way we treat others. What do you think it is?

Discuss these questions in groups, and report back to the class.

open-hearted enough to see God working in Jesus.

Jesus has a special concern for the outsiders (Zacchaeus was just one of many). The same concern has led John Smith, a present-day follower of Jesus, to give his time to Australia's bikers.

Can you think of any people in the Gospels who were not open, like Zacchaeus?

Zacchaeus saw that Jesus was a special kind of person. But what did that really mean? Who or what was he? If you have been brought up as a Christian, or if you know much about Christianity, you might think that this is a daft question. But it is a very important question.

Some of the closest people to Jesus were the twelve apostles. Their leader was Simon Peter. But the Gospels say that even they did not really know who Jesus was until Peter blurted it out one day.

`You are the Messiah,' he said.

Of course—that was it! Jesus was the one everybody had been waiting for—the one who would kick the Romans out of Israel and begin the Kingdom of God. You can imagine how

Zacchaeus, the tax collector from Jericho, was determined to see Jesus for himself. Because he was too short to see over the heads of the crowd, he climbed a tree. What took him by surprise was that Jesus should want to see him!

excited the apostles must have been.

But Jesus has a surprise in store for them. He *is* the Messiah, but not the sort of Messiah they expect. He begins to explain to them that he is going to suffer and die a terrible death. At first, the disciples are horrified. Peter even tries to contradict Jesus—but slowly they begin to learn. (You can read the story for yourselves in Matthew 16:13–23.)

Why were the disciples surprised when Jesus told them what was going to happen to him? Imagine you were one of them. Write a letter to a friend about your feelings. Here are some words you might find useful:

astonishment
disappointment
confusion
despair
fear

16

Seeing God in Jesus

Experience is a very powerful thing. When we experience things for ourselves, we begin to understand them better.

For instance, I know some things about New York. But if I went and lived there, I would know New York in a much deeper way.

● Can you think of any other examples like this?

● Why do teachers think that school trips are a good idea?

The Gospels say that three of Jesus' disciples—Peter, James and John—had an amazing experience. Jesus took them up to the top of a mountain to pray.

While Jesus was praying, and as the disciples watched, a change came over him. His face changed its appearance, and his clothes became dazzling white. Then, all of a sudden, the disciples saw two other figures with him: Moses and Elijah! Last of all, a cloud seemed to appear as if from nowhere, and a voice said: 'This is my Son, whom I have chosen: listen to him!'

Christians today call this incident the **Transfiguration**.

The Transfiguration was a very strange thing. The Gospels say that it confused and terrified the disciples even at the time. They already believed that Jesus was the Messiah. But this experience seemed to suggest something even more.

They had experienced Jesus for a moment in all his glory as the Son of God.

Can you think of another moment in Jesus' life when a voice from heaven is heard?

The Gospels tell us about the Transfiguration here. But the Transfiguration was not the only experience of Jesus the disciples had. Mark's Gospel was written in about AD64. By that time the disciples could look back over all the things which had happened to them. They had thought about them and had had time to work out what they meant. The Gospels themselves show us some of the conclusions they came to.

What were these experiences the disciples had? Here is a quick list:

They had seen Jesus perform miracles. He had healed the sick and raised the dead, and shown his power over nature.

They had seen him transfigured on the mountain.

He had prayed with them and looked after them.

He had taught them.

He had died a terrible death, and this had made them afraid and upset.

After they thought him dead and gone, they had found his tomb empty, and he had appeared to them alive again in love and joy.

They felt his presence with them as they prayed, and were given power themselves to teach and heal—and courage to suffer.

● They had seen many people becoming Christians, sharing their own experience and starting a new life.

All these things led the earliest Christians to a very important conclusion. Jesus was not just the Messiah. They began to see that God had acted in him in a special way—a way which was quite different from the way God had acted in other holy people in the past.

In fact, they said, Jesus was God himself, made man.

Many parts of the New Testament point to this belief, which is still central to Christianity today. The idea that God became a man in Jesus is called the **incarnation**.

John's Gospel begins with a very beautiful poem exploring the theme of the incarnation. The writer uses the idea of God's 'Word' to describe the nature of God in the person of Jesus:

'In the beginning was the Word, and the Word was with God, and the Word was God. He was in the beginning with God; all things were made through him, and without him was not anything made that was made. In him was life, and the life was the light of men...

'And the Word became flesh and dwelt among us, full of grace and truth; we have beheld his glory, glory as of the only Son from the Father.'

The idea of the incarnation helped Christians to understand many of the things they knew about Jesus. It would have helped them to understand the Transfiguration, for instance, and why Jesus was said never to have had a human father.

So, from very earliest times, Christians have said that they experienced God in three ways:

He is God the **Father**, the Father of Jesus and of all creation.

He is God the **Son**, who became a man in Jesus.

He is God the **Holy Spirit**, who guides his people, helps them make the right decisions, and fills them with his love.

Christians do not believe that there are three gods. They are clear that there is only one. But God is three-in-one: he is Father, Son and Holy Spirit. The idea of God as three-in-one is called the *Trinity*.

● St Patrick is supposed to have used a shamrock to explain the Trinity to the people of Ireland. How would it have helped them to understand it? What else do you think he could have used?

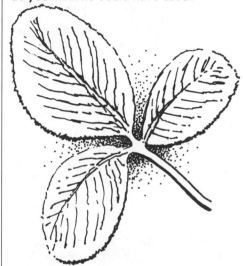

● Read the story of Jesus' baptism in Mark 1:9—11. It shows the Trinity at work. Match the first half of each sentence below with the correct second half.

The voice from heaven represents	the Son
Jesus is	the Holy Spirit
The dove represents	the Father

● Christians believe Jesus is both God and man. Look at each picture below. Does it stress his 'God side' or his 'man side'?

Right: The great east window tapestry by Graham Sutherland in Coventry Cathedral.
Below: This scene showing Jesus being taken down from the cross is sculptured at the top of a column in the cloister of the church at Santillana del Mar in Spain.
Bottom: A film version of the crucifixion: from the *Jesus Project*.

17

Jesus Calms a Storm

We have stories of Jesus doing some extraordinary things. It is not every day that someone is cured without seeing a doctor. Five loaves and two fish would not normally feed 5,000 people.

There are a great many miracle stories in the Gospels. But why? The Gospel writers had lots of stories about Jesus to choose from. No one Gospel includes all of them. All four of them together do not tell us everything about Jesus. We do not even know what he looked like, nor what happened to him between the ages of twelve and thirty. So why did the Gospel writers put in so many miracles?

The answer seems to be this. The miracle stories were important to the early Christians. They showed

● that Jesus cared about people.
● Jesus' power and authority.

● who Jesus is. (His power and authority have to come from somewhere!)

Many of the miracle stories are easy to understand. They are straight-forward. In others, the meaning is not so obvious.

In one story, Jesus calms a storm. It is worth looking at this miracle in detail. The version from Mark's Gospel (chapter 4, verses 35–41) is printed below. Read it carefully. Then look at the **notes** which follow. They deal with parts of the story which need a closer look. Try to work out possible answers to the questions they raise. You can do this on your own or in a group.

This story, like the feeding of the 5,000, is called a **nature miracle**. It shows Jesus' power over the forces of nature.

'On the evening of that same day Jesus said to his disciples, "Let us go across to the other side of the lake." So they left the crowd; the disciples got into the boat in which Jesus was already sitting, and they took him with them. Other boats were there too. Suddenly a strong wind blew up, and the waves began to spill over into the boat, so that it was about to fill with water. Jesus was in the back of the boat, sleeping with his head on a pillow. The disciples woke him up and said, "Teacher, don't you care that we are about to die?"

'Jesus stood up and commanded the wind, "Be quiet!" and he said to the waves, "Be still!" The wind died down, and there was a great calm. Then Jesus said to his disciples, "Why are you frightened? Have you still no faith?"

'But they were terribly afraid and said to one another, "Who is this man? Even the wind and the waves obey him!"'

NOTES

● The 'lake' in the story is Lake Galilee. Even today, it is very stormy. Without warning, violent winds can funnel through the hills around the lake. These whip up the waves and make conditions very dangerous for boats.

Does this help us understand the story? How?

● There is an interesting detail in verse 38. Jesus was asleep in the stern, 'with his head on a pillow'.

Why might the writer have included this detail?

● Jesus asks the disciples, 'Have you still no faith?'

Why does he ask this question?

● Episodes of television series often end with a 'cliffhanger'. The action breaks off just when you want it to continue. It makes you want to watch again next week. This miracle story ends with a sort of 'cliffhanger', too. The disciples ask, 'Who is this man? Even the wind and the waves obey him!' They do not find out until later.

In a way, the readers are being asked the question. What answer does the writer want them to give?

● The first readers of this story would have known the Old Testament, the Jewish Bible. Some parts of the Old Testament can act as clues to help us understand this story:

—God makes the universe in the Book of Genesis. Before he does so, his Spirit was said to be 'moving over the *water*'.

—The Jewish people were slaves in Egypt in the time of Moses. God set them free, and they left. (This was the *Exodus*.) On their way to the promised land of Israel, they had to cross the Red Sea. By a miracle, God made the *water* part for them.

—The Psalms in the Old Testament are poems and hymns to God. Psalm 107 talks about sailors in a storm. It says:

'In their trouble they called to the Lord, and he saved them from their distress. He calmed the raging storm, and the waves became quiet.'

● In the Old Testament, people are often afraid when God does something. For example, the people 'trembled with

The Gospels give many examples of Jesus' power over nature. Here he commands the calming of one of the fierce storms so common on Lake Galilee.

fear' when God gave Moses the Ten Commandments on Mount Sinai.

In what ways are these sections of the Old Testament like Jesus' miracle?

● The story's first readers knew the Old Testament. So they may well have remembered these sections.

When they read this miracle, what would it show them about Jesus?

● Life for the early Christians was often very stormy. They were persecuted (punished for their faith). In AD65, many of the Christians in Rome were executed by the Roman Emperor Nero.

How might this story have comforted them?

● Did Jesus really calm a storm? People who study the New Testament have different ideas. Here are three possible answers.

—The story is made up. The miracle does not help anyone, and it is very hard to believe. In a way, it does not matter. What the story *means* can still be true, even if Jesus never actually did it.

—The story is true. The writer checked his facts carefully. When he wrote, people were still alive who knew Jesus. He would have asked them, and they had no reason to lie.

—The story is partly true. The storm happened to stop just when Jesus told it to. It was all a coincidence.

Think of arguments *against* each of the three answers.

Which answer do you think is nearest the truth?

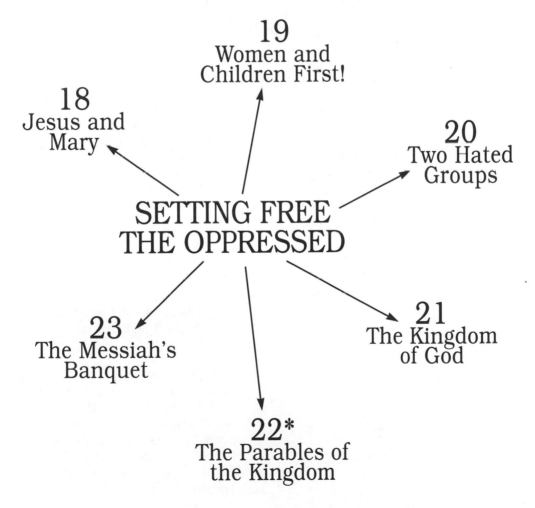

PART FOUR

19
Women and
Children First!

18
Jesus and
Mary

20
Two Hated
Groups

SETTING FREE
THE OPPRESSED

23
The Messiah's
Banquet

21
The Kingdom
of God

22*
The Parables of
the Kingdom

18

Jesus and Mary

Mary was the mother of Jesus. She is not often mentioned in the Gospels. The Gospel writers were mainly interested in writing about Jesus' preaching and teaching, when Mary seems to have been at home. We hear a lot more about Peter, for instance, than we do about her.

Luke and John tell us the most about Mary. The interesting thing is that, when she does appear, it is at very important moments.

● The whole story starts with Mary when she says she is willing to go through with the pregnancy (Luke 1:26–38).

● When Jesus is a baby, Mary meets a prophet called Simeon. He tells her that she will have to suffer (Luke 2:25–35).

● Jesus performs his first miracle because of something Mary says (John 2:1–11).

● Mary stands at the foot of the cross while Jesus is dying. Some of the last words Jesus says are to her (John 19:26–27).

Look up these stories in a Bible. What sort of person do you think Mary was?

Mary is very important for Catholic Christians today. They would say that she is more than Jesus' mother. She is the mother of all Christians. Let's explore one reason why they think this.

In John's story of the crucifixion, Jesus says to one of his disciples, 'Son, here is your mother.'

At first glance, this just looks as though Jesus is asking the disciple to look after Mary. But remember that the Gospel stories often have hidden meanings. In John's Gospel, this disciple (John calls him 'the beloved disciple') is used as a *special symbol*. He is a symbol of all Christians.

Jesus gives Mary to the disciple to be his mother. So in this view he is giving her to all Christians.

For this reason, Catholic Christians today believe that Mary is very close to them. But others disagree. Protestant Christians believe that if you concentrate too much on Mary, there is a danger you may forget God.

What do you think?

Something all Christians agree about is that Mary is an important example. They say she shows how God works through unexpected people. Think about it:

● Mary was a woman in a society ruled by men.

● Jewish people at that time thought that a woman's job was to marry and have children as soon as possible. But Mary was a virgin.

● Mary was poor. She had nowhere to stay in Bethlehem, and had to put her baby in an animals' feeding-trough.

Luke's Gospel says what Mary thought about these things. He tells us how she praised God in what we now call the 'Song of Mary' or the 'Magnificat'.

Mary takes her baby son to the Temple in Jerusalem, and Simeon predicts the suffering to come.

Here it is, from Luke 1:46–55:

'My heart praises the Lord;
my soul is glad because of God my
    Saviour,
for he has remembered me, his lowly
    servant!
From now on all people will call me
    happy,
because of the great things the Mighty
    God has done for me.
His name is holy;
from one generation to another
he shows mercy to those who honour him.
He has stretched out his mighty arm
and scattered the proud with all their
    plans.
He has brought down mighty kings from
    their thrones
and lifted up the lowly.
He has filled the hungry with good things,
and sent the rich away with empty hands.
He has kept the promise he made to our
    ancestors,
and has come to the help of his servant
    Israel.
He has remembered to show mercy to
    Abraham
and to all his descendants for ever!'

Look especially at the last few verses. Mary is saying that all the promises God had made in the Old Testament were about to come true in Jesus.

Answer the following questions:

● What was the name of the angel who appeared to Mary?

● Which two Gospels have the most about Mary in them?

● When did Jesus say, 'Mother, here is your son'?

● What other name is given to the Song of Mary?

● Mary does not appear very often in the Gospels. How do they show that she is important?

19

Women and Children First!

Imagine that you are going to start a new and powerful movement today. It could be any sort of movement—it doesn't have to be a religious one. You want it to spread all over the world.

● How would you go about it?

● How would you put across what you stood for?

● What sort of people would you want to get in touch with?

● What sort of people would you want as the movement's most important members?

Discuss these questions in your groups and try to come to some decisions. Each group will need a secretary to write these decisions down, and you must be prepared to give *reasons* for what you have decided.

Then EITHER write a group report to the rest of the class; OR make a wall display showing your conclusions in words and diagrams.

Are there any similarities between the decisions of the different groups in your class? What general conclusions can you draw?

The movement Jesus started has probably been the most successful the world has ever known. It has survived for 2,000 years so far, and has hundreds of millions of members today.

Millions more have been influenced by its teachings.

BUT

Jesus did not choose people who were

rich or powerful to be the first workers in his movement. He does not seem to have bothered to get in touch with famous or influential people.

Think about Jesus' first disciples. Who were they? What sort of jobs did they have? Would *you* have chosen them?

There is something surprising about a lot of Jesus' teaching. He seems to turn the world's ideas upside-down! The things that people usually consider important do not seem to have mattered to him. The people he chose for his movement first of all were the ordinary people, the poor and the sinful.

The Gospels say that even Jesus' disciples themselves had trouble understanding what Jesus was up to. Matthew's Gospel tells us about a time

Children are always quick to appear on the scene when anything exciting happens—and they were always part of the crowd around Jesus, sensing his welcome.

Name a sinner whom Jesus chose. Look back to chapter 15 to help you.

when they asked him about it straight out: 'Who *is* the greatest in the Kingdom of Heaven?' Here is the rest of the story (from Matthew 18:2–5):

'So Jesus called a child, made him stand in front of them, and said, "I assure you that unless you change and become like children, you will never enter the Kingdom of heaven. The greatest in the Kingdom of heaven is the one who humbles himself and becomes like this child. And whoever welcomes in my name one such child as this, welcomes me."'

Jesus seems to be saying, 'If you want to know what God thinks is really great, then look at a few children.'

There is another story in the Gospels which makes the same sort of point. Look it up for yourselves in Mark 10:13–16. It is very beautiful, and because of this it is often illustrated on Christian greetings cards and in pictures.

Make a list of some ideas about little children around the class. What are they like? Be honest!

Now look again carefully at the story from Matthew. Why does Jesus think his followers should be like them? This picture sequence should give you a clue.

Even when children have been naughty, they usually show loving trust in their parents. Jesus taught that his followers should have the same attitude

to God, their Father in heaven. That is the secret of true greatness.

When Jesus talked about children, he turned the ordinary values of the world upside-down. Children were often treated badly at the time of Jesus, and women were too. Their husbands could divorce them without their consent, and that meant they often lost all they possessed as well as being disgraced. Women could not be witnesses in court. They could not sit with the men in the synagogues.

But women have a very important place in the Gospel story, starting with Jesus' mother Mary, when she agrees to do what God wants and bear a son. Later, Jesus had women followers such as Martha and Mary, who were very close to him. He protected women by saying that people should not get divorced. The Gospels say that it was his women followers who were the first to find his tomb empty and who ran to tell the men disciples the astonishing news that he had risen from the dead.

We live in a world where people are sometimes deprived of what many of us enjoy because they are powerless or poor. The women and children in the Gospels can be seen to represent all who are powerless and poor in the world. Jesus' teachings, and the way he acted, show that everybody has a place in the Kingdom of God, and those the world values least are given a special welcome.

Jesus' attitude to women and children has often been described as *revolutionary*, because he challenged the ideas of his time. What do you think Jesus would want (or wants) to challenge in our society, and why? (Be careful! Just because Jesus was revolutionary about *some* things does not make *all* revolutions right!)

Read the story about Jesus and a woman in Mark 14:3–9, and answer these questions:

● Why were the people angry with the woman?

● Why does Jesus tell them to leave her alone?

● What does Jesus say the woman has anointed him for?

● How would you sum up the woman's attitude to Jesus?

● How would you sum up Jesus' attitude to her?

20
Two Hated Groups

Most Jews in Jesus' time hated the Romans. It is not difficult to imagine why.

Most of them also hated the Samaritans. We studied this group in chapter 10, 'Freedom from Old Ideas'. (Look back to this chapter to refresh your memory.)

What did Jesus think of these two hated groups?

THE SAMARITANS

● came from *Samaria*, the central area of Palestine;

● were no longer strict Jews;

● had a religion that was like Judaism, but not the same.

THE PARABLE OF THE GOOD SAMARITAN

This is one of Jesus' most famous parables. Luke's Gospel (chapter 10) says he told it to a teacher of the Jewish Law (Torah). This teacher—perhaps a Pharisee—wanted to know what he had to do to receive eternal life. Jesus asked him what the Torah commanded.

'Love the Lord your God with all your heart, with all your soul, with all your strength, and with all your mind, and love your neighbour as yourself,' the man answered.

Jesus said he was quite right. This was what he had to do. However, the man wanted to know who his 'neighbour' was. After all, it could be the person next door, or in the same town, or in the same country, or whatever.

Jesus' parable answered the man's question:

The Parable of the Good Samaritan shows

● *that Samaritans, or any other group of people, are valued by God like everybody else.* Hating them is wrong. One reason they were hated was because they were not pure Jews by blood. Racism was a problem in Jesus' time too.

● *how people should behave.* This is what 'loving your neighbour' means. (It does not mean 'going out with the person next door'!) It shows the right sort of attitude to have. So Jesus said to the teacher at the end of the story, 'You go, then, and do the same.'

Suppose Jesus told this story today. Write a modern version of the parable.
(Remember that part of the shock value of the story is making the hero a Samaritan! Who will you put in his place?)

'There was once a man who was going down from Jerusalem to Jericho when robbers attacked him, stripped him, and beat him up, leaving him half dead. It so happened that a priest was going down that road; but when he saw the man, he walked on by, on the other side. In the same way a Levite also came along, went over and looked at the man, and then walked on by, on the other side. But a Samaritan who was travelling that way came upon the man, and when he saw him, his heart was filled with pity. He went over to him, poured oil and wine on his wounds and bandaged them; then he put the man on his own animal and took him to an inn, where he took care of him. The next day he took out two silver coins and gave them to the innkeeper. "Take care of him," he told the innkeeper, "and, when I come back this way, I will pay you whatever else you spend on him."'

JESUS HEALS A ROMAN CENTURION'S SERVANT

A centurion was a Roman army officer who commanded one hundred men. The Gospels say that a centurion asked Jesus to heal his servant, who was seriously ill.

Jesus decided to go with him, but the centurion said, 'No sir. I do not deserve to have you come into my house. Just give the order, and my servant will get well. I, too, am a man under the authority of superior officers, and I have soldiers under me. I order this one, "Go!" and he goes; and I order

The Roman army controlled Palestine in Jesus' day, and army officers (centurions) often come into the Gospel story. The centurion pictured on this gravestone now in the Colchester and Essex Museum was part of the Roman force which occupied Britain.

that one, "Come!" and he comes; and I order my slave, "Do this!" and he does it.'

This surprised Jesus. The centurion was used to his own orders being obeyed, and expected Jesus' orders to be obeyed too. 'I have never found anyone in Israel with faith like this,' Jesus said. 'Go home, and what you believe will be done for you.'

The centurion's servant was healed that very moment.

The Romans were the Jews' enemies: the invaders who had conquered their country. And here was Jesus helping one of them! The story shows that the Romans, like the Samaritans, are people too. They should therefore be cared for like anyone else.

Jesus said in another place,

'Love your enemies; do good to those who hate you.'

● Why does Jesus say the centurion has faith?

● What are these two stories teaching about God? Think *carefully* through them, and make a list of ideas.

● What do the stories suggest our attitude should be towards people of different backgrounds?

21
The Kingdom of God

Nearly 600 years before Jesus, the Jews fought a terrible war. This was against the Babylonians, who had invaded Israel. The Jews lost, and became part of the Babylonian Empire.

Invasions, war and conquest continued. After the Babylonians came the Persians, then the Greeks. There was a brief spell of independence when the Jews ruled themselves, then the Romans arrived. By Jesus' time, the Jews had been ruled by foreigners for most of the last 600 years. They had had enough.

They did not want more foreign rulers. They wanted God to be in charge.

But this meant different things to different Jews:

● The **Zealots** thought that if God were in charge, the Jews would be in charge. There would be a war against their enemies, the Romans, led by the Messiah. The war would win them a new Jewish empire.

● The **Essenes** thought that if God were in charge, all evil would be wiped out. Evil spirits and evil people would be destroyed.

● Some people thought the whole thing was daft. The **Sadducees** thought like this. They were a small group.
—Many of them were priests in the Temple.
—Some were very rich.
—They only believed in ideas in the Torah (the first five books of the Bible).
—They did not believe in life after death, angels, or the Messiah.
—They were at the top of the tree in society, and did not want trouble with the Romans because that might affect their power.

Most people, then, wanted

God in charge.

The name given to this idea is

the Kingdom of God.

When Jesus started his work, he said:

'The right time has come, and the Kingdom of God is near! Turn away from your sins and believe the Good News!' (Mark 1:15)

So Jesus was saying that God would soon be in charge. But this had nothing to do with war or violence. God, not human beings, would rule.

Jesus said the Kingdom was like a seed growing into a plant. God makes the seed grow, and he makes the Kingdom come. Look this parable up in Mark 4:26–29.

Many people in Jesus' day wanted God to be in charge (God's Kingdom) in place of the Roman authorities. Here Roman soldiers mingle in the crowd surrounding the man who claimed to be the Messiah.

The Kingdom of God did not just mean that God was in charge. The Kingdom would be made up of

God's new people.

● Anyone could join God's new people. You did not have to be a Jew. You did not have to be important. Non-Jews (Gentiles) and the 'bad characters' Jesus met (outcasts) could join.

● God's new people would be God's new people for ever. The Kingdom is a community of people who belong to God and Jesus, and who share their life. That community will survive death.

People in the Kingdom are expected to behave in a certain way. Jesus summed this up when he said to his followers:

> 'I give you a new commandment: love one another. As I have loved you, so you must love one another.' (John 13:34)

Think back to the Parable of the Good Samaritan. That showed what this 'love' was. It was more than just a feeling. It did not mean 'being in love with someone' either (although that is no bad thing!).

The sort of love Jesus means here leads to action. It is to do with caring about others, especially people who are poor, ill or helpless. But it is available to anyone.

When Jesus was asked which was the most important of the command-ments in God's Law (the Torah), he replied:

> 'The most important one is this, "Listen, Israel! The Lord our God is the only Lord. Love the Lord your God with all your heart, with all your soul, with all your mind, and with all your strength." The second most important commandment is this: "Love your neighbour as you love yourself." There is no other commandment more important than these two.' (Mark 12:29–31)

And Jesus said that this sort of love sums up the teaching of the Old Testament. This rule of behaviour is known as the

Golden Rule.

> 'Treat others as you would like them to treat you. This is the meaning of the Law and the Prophets.'

● **Answer the following questions in your own words:**

What does 'Kingdom of God' mean?

Why did the Jews want the Kingdom of God to arrive?

What did a) the Zealots
**　　　　　b) the Essenes**
**　　　　　c) the Sadducees**
think about the Kingdom of God?

Who did Jesus say could join the Kingdom of God?

How long would they be members?

● Look again at the Golden Rule.

How would people carry it out if
    —they were told to help wash up?
    —their friends were talking behind
    someone's back?
    —they saw someone being bullied?
    —they knew that people were starving?
    —there was an election coming?

The answers are not always easy.

● In chapters 5–7 of Matthew's Gospel is a collection of Jesus' teaching. It is sometimes called the Sermon on the Mount. In part of the sermon, Jesus refers to what the Torah says, and then gives his own teaching. In Matthew's Gospel, look up what Jesus says about
    —murder (5:21—22);
    —adultery (5:27—28);
    —revenge (5:38–40);
    —how we should treat our enemies (5:43–45).

You will see that his teaching is very strict and demanding. If you have time, copy and complete the table below. (What the Torah said will be introduced by something like, 'You have heard that it was said.')

Subject	What the Torah said	What Jesus said
1. Murder		
2. Adultery		
3. Revenge		
4. Enemies		

22*
The Parables of the Kingdom

The Gospels often show Jesus teaching people. He taught his disciples, and he taught the crowds who came out to hear him as he went about the towns and villages.

Jesus taught about the Kingdom of God. In this chapter we will be looking at how he went about it, as well as exploring a little of what he taught.

One of the best ways to help people to understand a new idea is to tell them that it is a bit like something they already know about. For instance, if someone asked me what plain chocolate was like, I might begin by saying, 'Well, it's like milk chocolate, only it's darker.' Notice that I have done two things:

● I have started with something the other person already knows from *his or her experience.*

● I have made a *comparison* between the thing already known about and the new thing I want to describe.

Have you ever been helped to understand something in this way? What was it?

Teachers spend a lot of time trying to think up good comparisons. Try it for yourself. What would you say the following things were like, if you were talking to somebody who did not know anything about them:

● having a brother or sister
● baking a cake
● putting on lipstick
● newspapers
● a computer
● swimming

Try to keep your comparisons as simple as possible. And try to imagine the *needs* and *experience* of the person to whom you are talking.

Jesus used this technique in teaching about the Kingdom of God. When he taught, he told stories which *made comparisons* between the Kingdom of God and something else.

These comparison-stories Jesus told are called **parables**. Some of them were remembered and written down in our Gospels. Occasionally they are quite long, but others are very short. We are going to look at an example of each. Both are from Mark's Gospel.

PARABLE 1: THE MUSTARD SEED

'What shall we say the Kingdom of God is like?' asked Jesus. 'What parable shall we use to explain it? It is like this. A man takes a mustard seed, the smallest seed in the world, and plants it in the ground. After a while it grows up and becomes the biggest of all plants. It puts out such large branches that the birds come and make their nests in its shade.' (Mark 4:30–32)

Look carefully at this parable.

How does it begin? How can we tell that Jesus is going to make a comparison?

What does it tell us about the people who listened to Jesus? Were they

● interested in skateboarding?
● used to a life of farming in the countryside?
● deep-sea divers?

So what does the parable mean? Sometimes this can be quite a difficult question to answer! But there are a few things to notice. Jesus is saying that the Kingdom of God may have small beginnings, but it is going to grow and grow. Perhaps the disciples were feeling discouraged, and Jesus gave them this parable to cheer them up. Or perhaps people had been making fun of them. They should not worry. Eventually the Kingdom is going to be so big that all sorts of people will come and join it. These are the 'birds' at the end of the story.

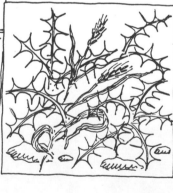

PARABLE 2: THE SOWER

This is a very well known parable, but it is quite hard to understand at first sight (Mark 4:3–8). The Gospels give us an explanation a little while after they have told it. The sower is sowing God's message, and the types of ground are different types of people.

● Some people are like the seed falling on the path. As soon as they hear God's message, the Devil (the birds) snatches it away.

● Some people are like the seeds on rocky ground. They start off all right, but the message does not really sink in, and they soon give up.

● Some people are like the seeds sown among thorn bushes. They start off well too, but soon they get so taken up with making good and with their own worries that they give up hearing God for other things.

● Some people are like the seeds sown in good soil. They really accept the message and it begins to 'bear fruit'!

Maybe we have all seen people take something up in a burst of enthusiasm, only to drop it a little while later. Perhaps we have done something like this ourselves! In the Parable of the Sower, Jesus is saying that the same thing can happen to God's message about the Kingdom. Some people will not listen. Others listen for a while and then get bored. But eventually the people who take what God wants to heart will find an enormous reward.

Both of the parables we have been looking at in this chapter speak about something good that will happen in the future. Still today, Christians do not think about the Kingdom as something which happened in the past. They see it beginning to happen here and now, and they look forward in *hope* to a time when God's promises will be completely fulfilled.

Jesus told the Parable of the Mustard Seed using picture language about farming. Try to retell it using different picture language, but keeping the same message. You will need to give it a new title.

The Messiah's Banquet

Most of us probably have some idea of what heaven might be like. Look at these four pictures.

● Do they have anything in common?

● How do they change as the characters get older?

OOH! I THINK HE'S HEAVEN.

MY MUMMY SAYS MY TORTOISE HAS GONE TO HEAVEN!

● What is *traditional* about the picture of the little boy's tortoise?

Most of the Jews of Jesus' time believed in heaven. Like us, they had traditional ways of talking about it. They thought of heaven as a huge party given by God. The Messiah would be there, and so would the great heroes of Judaism such as Abraham, Isaac and Jacob. The guests would be all the people who had obeyed the Torah and so done what God wanted.

We call this idea of a huge party in heaven the **Messiah's banquet**.

When Jesus talked about heaven he used the idea of the Messiah's banquet, like most other people. Luke's Gospel tells us that one day he went to eat at the house of one of the most important Pharisees. There were some other guests as well and, after they had all taken their places around the table, they started talking. By now Jesus was well known as a teacher and a holy man.

One of the guests seems to have wanted to impress him:

'How happy are those who will sit down at the feast in the Kingdom of God!' he said.

What sort of a reaction do you think the man was expecting from Jesus?

Jesus replied by telling him a story, which is sometimes called the Parable of the Great Feast. Here it is, from Luke 14:16–24:

'There was once a man who was giving a great feast to which he invited many people. When it was time for the feast, he sent his servant to tell his guests, "Come, everything is ready!" But they all began,

HEAVEN MUST BE LIKE BEING IN LOVE.

I'M LOOKING FORWARD TO SEEING MY FRIENDS AGAIN.

one after another, to make excuses. The first one told the servant, "I have bought a field and must go and look at it; please accept my apologies." Another one said, "I have bought five pairs of oxen and am on my way to try them out; please accept my apologies." Another one said, "I have just got married, and for that reason I cannot come."

'The servant went back and told all this to his master. The master was furious and said to his servant, "Hurry out to the streets and alleys of the town, and bring back the poor, the crippled, the blind, and the lame." Soon the servant said, "Your order has been carried out, sir, but there is room for more." So the master said to the servant, "Go out to the country roads and lanes and make people come in, so that my house will be full. I tell you all that none of those men who were invited will taste my dinner!"'

Look at the parable carefully. Each part is meant to stand for something else.

● **Who is the man giving the feast?**

● **What is the feast?**

● **What is meant to be surprising in the parable?**

The Pharisees thought that they had got religious things pretty well worked out. They were fairly certain in their own minds about the sort of people who

Jesus at dinner with his friends: this is the picture behind the idea of the Messiah's banquet—heaven seen as a huge party given by God.

would be going to heaven. For many of them, religion was simply a matter of keeping rules. As long as you did that, they thought, you would be all right. Many of them thought it was perfectly possible to combine being religious with being rich and successful, and not taking very much care of the poor or showing anyone very much love.

So the Pharisees thought they were fine. They would be the guests at the Messiah's banquet. But Jesus seems to be saying that the kind of people who think they are certain of a place in heaven should not be so sure. They are too wrapped up in their own affairs—with the latest things they have bought and with their own relationships. They are pretending to be religious, but really they are putting these things in the place where God ought to be.

In another parable, Jesus talks about people being so busy with their own affairs that it stops them from doing what God wants. Which one? (You can turn back to chapter 22 to help you.)

So, who does Jesus say will be at the Messiah's banquet? Look at the parable again. They will be:

● the poor
● the crippled
● the blind
● the lame.

Of course Jesus does not mean only the disabled will be there! These were all people who were shut out from the 'best' society. They were even blamed for their own suffering because people thought

God was punishing them. Once again, Jesus is turning the values of his time upside-down. Nobody is cut off from God's invitation to the Messiah's banquet—except people who think they have a right to be there and who live wicked lives.

How do you think the other guests in the Pharisee's house felt about what Jesus had to say? Write a letter from one of them to his friend, describing what happened and his feelings about it.

Jesus did not just teach about what the Messiah's banquet would be like. In one of his most famous miracles he acted it out. The Feeding of the Five Thousand is the only miracle story we have which is in all four Gospels. (Perhaps that shows us how important the earliest Christians thought it was.) Here is the story as Luke tells it, in chapter 9:12–17. Jesus has spent the day teaching the people about the Kingdom of God:

'When the sun was beginning to set, the twelve disciples came to him and said, "Send the people away so that they can go to the villages and farms round here and find food and lodging, because this is a lonely place."

'But Jesus said to them, "You yourselves give them something to eat."

'They answered, "All we have are five loaves and two fish. Do you want us to go and buy food for this whole crowd?" (There were about five thousand men there.)

'Jesus said to his disciples, "Make the

people sit down in groups of about fifty each."

'After the disciples had done so, Jesus took the five loaves and two fish, looked up to heaven, thanked God for them, broke them, and gave them to the disciples to distribute to the people. They all ate and had enough, and the disciples took up twelve baskets of what was left over.'

This is an astonishing story. Some people find it very hard to believe—but others have no trouble with it. They would say that if Jesus could heal the sick and raise the dead, why shouldn't he be able to feed people like this?

But the point is that when Jesus did it, and when people of his time were told about it, everybody would immediately think of the idea of the Messiah's banquet. The Messiah is there—Jesus—and he is sharing food with his people. It is as though the banquet of heaven has already started.

We will be looking at some of these ideas again when we study the Last Supper in chapter 26.

● What do you think of the idea of heaven as a huge banquet or meal? You will need to think about the people you regularly eat with at home, and what people do on special occasions.

● Suppose Jesus was living in our country today, as he was in Palestine all that time ago. Who do you think he would say were to be guests at the Messiah's banquet now, and why?

● Write a drama sketch of the Parable of the Great Feast. You might like to practise it and perform it to the rest of your class, or in assembly.

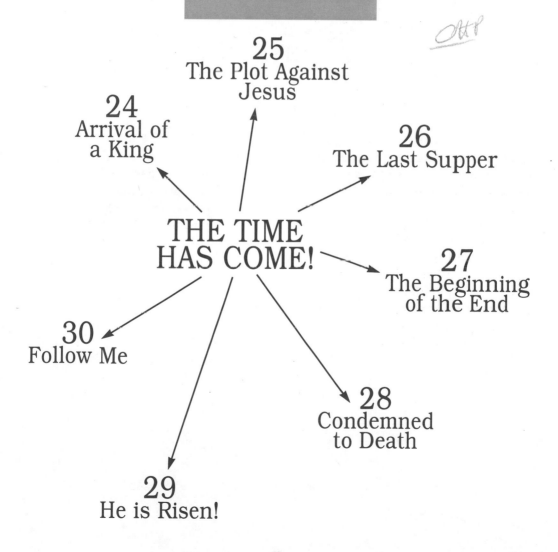

PART
FIVE

25
The Plot Against
Jesus

24
Arrival of
a King

26
The Last Supper

THE TIME
HAS COME!

27
The Beginning
of the End

30
Follow Me

28
Condemned
to Death

29
He is Risen!

24
Arrival
of a King

When someone has done something spectacular or successful, people often want to share in the triumph.

● Supporters crowd to greet a football team who have won (or even come third!) in the World Cup.

● Fans gather at an airport to catch a glimpse of music's latest idol as she arrives.

● People come in their thousands to line the coach's route for a royal wedding.

When Jesus came into Jerusalem on a donkey, the crowds were there.

He had made arrangements beforehand. Outside the city, he told his disciples to go into a nearby village. 'As you go in,' he said, 'you will find a colt tied up that has never been ridden. Untie it and bring it here. If someone asks you why you are untying it, tell him that the Master needs it.'

It is unlikely that Jesus knew where the donkey was because he had special powers. He had probably asked the owner if he could borrow it. The

Palm leaves

disciples found the animal, and brought it to Jesus. They spread their cloaks on its back before Jesus got on. He rode towards the capital.

In the Old Testament, the prophet Zechariah had said:

> 'Rejoice, rejoice, people of Zion!
> Shout for joy, you people of Jerusalem!
> Look, your king is coming to you!
> He comes triumphant and victorious,
> but humble and riding on a donkey.'
> (Zechariah, 9:9)

The people in Jerusalem seem to have remembered this. They came out to meet their king. They laid their cloaks down on the road in front of him, and waved palm branches they had cut down from the trees. 'God bless him who comes in the name of the Lord!' they shouted with the disciples. 'God bless the coming kingdom of King David, our father! Praise God!'

When the Pharisees heard it, they told Jesus to tell his followers to be

The outer courtyard of the Temple was the one place non-Jews might enter. But cheating traders had taken it over. Jesus exploded with anger at what he saw. God's house was meant to be a place of prayer.

quiet. 'I tell you that if they keep quiet, the stones themselves will start shouting,' he replied.

Jesus went to the Temple, and was furious with what he saw. *Jesus clearing the temple*

● People were making money out of the worshippers:

—Animals for sacrifice had to be perfect. Traders were selling them for a high price.

—Each Jew had to pay a tax to keep the Temple going. It had to be paid in the special Temple coinage. No other currency would do. The moneychangers were making a huge profit from changing Roman coins for Jewish ones.

● For the Jews, the Temple was the holiest place in the world. Yet some were using it as a short cut between one part of the city and another.

The market was in the Court of the Gentiles. (See the diagram in chapter 11.) This was the only part of the Temple where non-Jews were allowed. Making money was more important than letting the Gentiles worship God!

Jesus overturned the dealers' tables and threw them out. He would not allow anyone to use the Temple as a short cut. He told people what God had said in the Old Testament: 'My Temple will be called a house of prayer for the people of all nations.'

And he added, 'You have turned it into a hideout for thieves!'

The day Jesus entered Jerusalem is called Palm Sunday. The Palm Sunday service is special in many Christian churches, where palm crosses (crosses made from palms) are given out. Some Christians walk round the church or process through the streets to remember the welcome the people gave Jesus. They may sing hymns, or even have a donkey with them in the procession.

Palm Sunday is the first day of **Holy Week**. Holy Week remembers Jesus' suffering and death (**passion**), and the things which led up to this. Holy Week includes:

—Palm Sunday
—Maundy Thursday
—Good Friday
—Holy Saturday

The next day, after Holy Week is over, is Easter Day.

Crosses like this, made from a single palm frond, are given out at many churches on Palm Sunday—a reminder of the palm branches strewn in Jesus' path on the day he rode in triumph into Jerusalem.

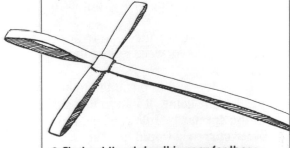

● Find out the dates this year for these days in Holy Week. (Most diaries will tell you.)

● Find out what each day remembers. (This book will help you!)

● You are a reporter for the *Jerusalem Independent*. Using the headline 'King or Criminal?' write an account of what happened when Jesus arrived in Jerusalem and went to the Temple.

● The Pharisees watched Jesus' arrival in Jerusalem. In John's Gospel (12:19), they say to each other, 'We are not succeeding at all! Look, the whole world is following him!' Mark's Gospel says the Jewish leaders 'began looking for some way to kill Jesus' after he threw the dealers out of the Temple.

The things Jesus did made them very angry. But why?

● Both the Jewish leaders and Jesus get angry. Anger can cause a lot of harm.

When is it right to be angry? When is it wrong?

Work out some ideas in small groups. Share your findings with the rest of the class.

25

The Plot Against Jesus

A lot of people wanted to follow Jesus. The Gospels say that crowds came out to see him wherever he went. People brought their sick friends and relatives to him, and crowds welcomed him when he rode into Jerusalem.

But right from the beginning Jesus had enemies as well. Matthew's Gospel says that King Herod even wanted him killed when he was a baby. In that story, Herod was frightened because the Wise Men had told him about a new king of the Jews who was born at Bethlehem. Herod wanted to make certain that he stayed king, so he ordered his soldiers to kill all the baby boys in Bethlehem who were under two years old. What Herod did sounds too horrible to believe, but we know that he was a very cruel ruler. He was certainly capable of things like this.

● How would you describe Herod's reasons for being afraid of Jesus? Were they: political, emotional, or a mixture of both?

● How did Joseph and Mary save Jesus in the story? Look back to chapter 3 to refresh your memory.

Jesus still had enemies once he was grown up. The main ones were:

● a large number of Pharisees;
● the Sadducees;
● Judas Iscariot.

Let's explore why each of these disliked Jesus.

Many of the **Pharisees** disliked Jesus because he upset the way they thought about religion. Remember that, for the

103

Pharisees, the holiest thing in the universe was the Torah, the Law of Moses. It was a kind of *bridge* between God and the world. They thought that

all the sadness and unfairness in the world was caused by sin. But God had given the Torah so that people would know how to do good. They would please God if they obeyed the Torah—and after they died, they would be guests in his Kingdom.

The Pharisees thought that Jesus disobeyed the Torah. In particular, he healed people on the Sabbath, when no work was meant to be done. Sometimes he went even further, and actually added to the Torah. Look back to chapter 21 to see how he did this in the Sermon on the Mount.

What Jesus said and did seemed terribly dangerous to many of the Pharisees. They had spent many years teaching the people in the synagogues about the Torah, sending missionaries abroad, and studying the Law of Moses.

Now Jesus was upsetting it all! Who was he, anyway? He wasn't even a proper rabbi! When the Pharisees asked him where he thought he got his authority from, he would not tell them. He thought they should be able to work it out for themselves.

The Gospels say that, as the opposition to Jesus grew, the Pharisees watched him more and more closely. When some of them saw him heal people on the Sabbath, they decided that they had had enough. They began to plot his death.

Jesus himself did not think that the Torah was a lot of nonsense. But he thought that the Kingdom of God was more important. Not all the Pharisees hated him. Some of them, like Nicodemus and Joseph of Arimathea, were interested in his ideas and even became his followers.

Imagine that you have been brought up as a Pharisee at the time of Jesus. You have heard him preach and think you might want to become one of his disciples. What problems would you have? How would you feel? Discuss this in class.

Now, on your own: Write a letter to a friend explaining your hopes and your doubts.

The **Sadducees** were the ruling party of the Jews. Their base was in Jerusalem. The Sadducees do not seem to have been as bothered as the Pharisees about Jesus' religious teachings (although they probably did not like what he said about the Torah, either).

They were interested in keeping on good terms with the Romans. Jesus seemed like a trouble-maker to them. A large number of people were following him about. He had entered Jerusalem like a king. If things got out of hand, who knew what might happen! The Romans might decide to take action, and people would be killed. The Sadducees might very well be blamed. Jesus was better off safely out of the way, in his grave.

The Sadducees' leader was the High Priest, Caiaphas. John's Gospel tells us that he suggested to the Sanhedrin (the Jewish Council) that it was better for one man to die than for the whole nation to be destroyed.

So there were Pharisees and

We know that Judas, one of Jesus' closest friends, betrayed him to his enemies for thirty silver coins. But what made him do it?

Sadducees who wanted to get rid of Jesus. The question was how to go about it. After all, Jesus was a popular man.

His enemies got their lucky chance when Judas Iscariot—one of Jesus' closest disciples—decided to betray him. We do not really know why he did this, but here are some possible explanations:

● The Devil suggested it to him. This is what the Gospels of Luke and John say.

● He did it for the money. The Sanhedrin gave him thirty pieces of silver as a reward for handing Jesus over to them. John's Gospel says that Judas was known to be unreliable about money. He had been helping himself to the funds Jesus and the apostles shared.

● He was disappointed in Jesus. 'Iscariot' might mean something like 'Zealot'. If Judas had joined Jesus because he thought he would be a warrior Messiah, he might have turned against him when he realized Jesus had other ideas.

Discuss which of these possible reasons you think is the most convincing. Or could it have been a mixture of all three? Write down your conclusions—remember to give reasons for what you have decided.

Whatever Judas' reasons were, he soon regretted what he had done. Matthew's Gospel says that after Jesus had been condemned to death, Judas hanged himself. There is another account of this in the Acts of the Apostles.

So Jesus' enemies eventually ganged up against him and had him crucified. We will be dealing with the rest of the story in the chapters that follow.

26

The Last Supper

Crowds of people welcomed Jesus when he arrived in Jerusalem. They had gone there to take part in the Jewish festival of **Passover**.

Passover is still a very important feast for Jews today. It is a celebration of how God rescued them from slavery in Egypt. That happened at the time of Moses, twelve-and-a-half centuries before Jesus.

At Jesus' time, as many people as could manage it would make the long journey to Jerusalem for Passover. They would go with their families to take part in the religious celebrations. The central part of these was a **special meal**. Its rules were laid down in the Torah. Each family would take a lamb to the Temple, where it was killed as a sacrifice to thank God for what he had done. Then the meat would be taken back to where they were staying, where it was cooked and eaten, along with other special

foods. These included **bread** and **wine**.

By keeping the Passover, the Jews showed that they were the people of God. They had a special relationship—a **covenant**—with him.

Jesus went to Jerusalem with his disciples to celebrate the Passover. The Gospels tell us about a meal they all ate together. This was the last time Jesus ate with the disciples before he died, and so we call it the **Last Supper**. It is very important for Christians today.

Jesus did a very surprising thing at the Last Supper. Here is the story from Matthew's Gospel (chapter 26:26–28):

> 'While they were eating, Jesus took a piece of bread, gave a prayer of thanks, broke it, and gave it to his disciples. "Take and eat it," he said; "this is my body."
> 'Then he took a cup, gave thanks to

Ever since their dramatic escape from Egypt, led by Moses, the Jewish people have celebrated Passover.

Top: Film still. *Bottom:* A Yemenite family sharing the Passover meal today.

> God, and gave it to them. "Drink it, all of you," he said; "this is my blood, which seals God's covenant, my blood poured out for many for the forgiveness of sins."'

This is very difficult to understand, but here are some ideas to help you:

● Jesus knows he is going to die. He breaks the bread and says, 'This is my body.' His body is going to be broken on the cross.

● Bread and wine were important parts of the Passover meal. They symbolized God's relationship with his people—the covenant. Jesus says that the wine is his blood. His blood will be shed when he is crucified. That is going to start a **new covenant**, a new relationship with a new people of God!

● Remember that the Jews believed the Kingdom of God would be like a meal with the Messiah—the 'Messiah's banquet'. What Jesus does here looks forward to what will happen then. It is a kind of foretaste of the Kingdom.

● Long ago God saved the Jews from slavery in Egypt. The Jews remembered this in a special way by sacrificing a lamb at Passover. They had other sacrifices as well, and some of these were to take away sins. Now it is Passover time again, but this time there is going to be a new sort of sacrifice— Jesus himself. He says that his blood is going to be poured out 'for the forgiveness of sins'. For this reason, John's Gospel calls him 'the Lamb of God'. His death is going to do something wonderful.

It was at a Passover meal that Jesus told his followers he was about to give his life (his body and blood) for the forgiveness of humankind. Christians today remember this in the Eucharist (or Breaking of Bread).

Catholic Christians call the Eucharist 'the Mass'. They believe that Jesus is really present at the Mass in the appearance of bread and wine. The ritual of the Mass is complicated and beautiful, and emphasizes how holy it is. A priest takes the service.

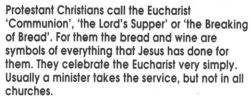

Protestant Christians call the Eucharist 'Communion', 'the Lord's Supper' or 'the Breaking of Bread'. For them the bread and wine are symbols of everything that Jesus has done for them. They celebrate the Eucharist very simply. Usually a minister takes the service, but not in all churches.

Christians often meet together for the **Eucharist** (a Greek word which means 'thanksgiving'.) At this service, bread and wine are taken and blessed, and then everybody eats and drinks a little of each. Christians have done this from the very earliest days in obedience to Jesus' words, 'Do this in memory of me.' (Luke 22:19) We know that they did it before the New Testament was even written down! The Eucharist is a very important act of worship. For most Christians it stands at the heart of their faith.

Finally, John's Gospel has some words of Jesus in it which help Christians to understand the Eucharist. These are some of them: read them for yourselves.

'I am the bread of life. He who comes to me will never be hungry; he who believes in me will never be thirsty.' (John 6:35)

'I am telling you the truth: if you do not eat the flesh of the Son of Man and drink his blood, you will not have life in yourselves. Whoever eats my flesh and drinks my blood has eternal life, and I will raise him to life on the last day. For my flesh is the real food; my blood is the real drink. Whoever eats my flesh and drinks my blood lives in me, and I live in him.' (John 6:53–56)

● Fill in the missing words in this passage. The list below it will help you.

Jesus ate a_____meal with his disciples at _____time. He took_____ and_____, and said they were his _____ and_____. Today we call this meal the _____._____ remember it in a special service called the_____.

Eucharist, last, body, Passover, bread, blood, Last Supper, Christians, disciples, wine.

● Here are some quick questions for you to answer:

What do Jews remember at Passover time?
What animal was sacrificed at Passover?
Why does John's Gospel call Jesus 'the Lamb of God'?
What does 'covenant' mean?

● If you have never been to a Christian Eucharist, try to go to one and watch. You can find out the time of the service from the notice-board of a local church, or ask your teacher to help you. (You will not want to offend anybody, so make sure you know what parts of the service you are allowed to join in before you go. Some churches are more strict about this than others. If you are not sure, ask the priest or minister before the service starts.)

● Talk to an adult Christian about what the Eucharist means to him or her. You might like to tape-record the interview as a radio programme. Present your findings to the rest of the class.

Revision.

27

The Beginning of the End

After the Last Supper, Jesus took Peter, James and John to Gethsemane. This was an olive grove outside Jerusalem. Jesus knew he was going to be crucified. The thought filled him with horror.

He left them to keep watch. 'The sorrow in my heart is so great that it almost crushes me,' he told them. He went away and prayed: 'Father, all things are possible for you. Take this cup of suffering from me. Not my will, however, but your will be done.'

While he was praying, the disciples fell asleep. He woke them up. 'Stay awake. Pray that you will not fall into temptation.' Jesus knew that Judas, his betrayer, was on his way.

Then Judas arrived with a band of armed men. 'The man I kiss is the one you want,' he told them. 'Arrest him!' He went up to Jesus. 'Hail, Master!' he said, and kissed him.

They seized him, and a fight started. Peter lashed out with his sword, and cut off the ear of Malchus, the High Priest's slave. 'Put your sword back!' Jesus ordered him, and said to the crowd, 'Did you have to come with swords and clubs, as though I were an outlaw? I was with you in the Temple every day, and you did not try to arrest me. But this is your hour to act, when the power of darkness rules.'

They took him to the High Priest's house, and the disciples fled.

Annas saw Jesus first. Annas was the father-in-law of the High Priest Caiaphas, and used to be High Priest himself.

Outside, it was a cold night. The servants and guards had made a charcoal fire by the gate. Peter had followed Jesus at a distance, and stood by the fire, keeping warm. A servant girl thought she recognized him. 'Aren't you

Jesus, escorted by the Temple guards, is led to the High Priest's house for trial.

also one of that man's disciples?' she asked. 'I don't know what you're talking about,' Peter replied. As he spoke, a cock crowed.

Annas questioned Jesus about his disciples and his teaching. 'I have always spoken publicly,' Jesus said. 'I have never said anything in secret. Why, then, do you question me? Question the people who heard me.'

One of the guards slapped Jesus in the face. 'Is that how you speak to the High Priest?' he said.

'If I have said anything wrong, tell everyone here what it was,' said Jesus. 'But if I am right in what I have said, why do you hit me?'

Annas sent Jesus to appear before Caiaphas and the whole of the Sanhedrin.

The Sanhedrin tried to find some

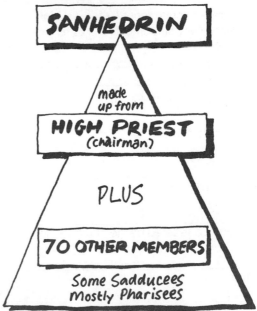

SANHEDRIN

made up from

HIGH PRIEST (chairman)

PLUS

70 OTHER MEMBERS

Some Sadducees Mostly Pharisees

The Sanhedrin was the Jewish Council. The Romans allowed the Sanhedrin to look after religious matters. It could also act as a criminal court in some cases.

evidence against Jesus. Witnesses lied about him. But their stories did not agree, so the evidence was useless. Some said Jesus had spoken against the Temple, saying he would destroy it. This evidence was confused. (Jesus had predicted the Temple would be destroyed, but had not said he would do it!)

'Have you no answer to the accusation they bring against you?' Caiaphas asked Jesus. Jesus stayed silent, and the High Priest realized they were getting nowhere. 'In the name of the living God, I now put you on oath: tell us if you are the Messiah, the Son of God,' he said.

'I am,' Jesus replied.

In his eyes, Jesus had blasphemed (insulted God). 'We don't need any more witnesses!' he told the Sanhedrin. 'What is your decision?'

The verdict was clear: Jesus was guilty and should be put to death.

Someone blindfolded Jesus. People spat in his face and hit him. 'Play the prophet now!' they jeered.

In the courtyard outside, the servant girl was talking to the others round the fire, while Peter watched. 'He is one of them,' she said. Peter denied it. One of the men had noticed Peter's northern accent. 'You can't deny that you are one of them,' he said. 'You, too, are from Galilee.'

Peter denied

'I swear that I am telling the truth!' Peter exclaimed. 'I do not know that man!' A cock crowed again. Peter suddenly remembered what Jesus had told him at the Last Supper: 'Before the cock crows twice tonight, you will say three times that you do not know me.' And he burst into tears.

Below is a 'court record' of Jesus' trial before the Sanhedrin. Fill it in as fully as you can.

Name of the accused:

Occupation:

Place of birth:

Evidence considered by the court:

Crime:

Verdict:

What do the disciples—especially Peter— do in the story here?

● **How well do you think they behave?**

● **Why do think they behave like this?**

The High Priest had what he wanted.

Condemned to Death

Trial before Pilate

The Romans did not allow the Jews to execute criminals. The Sanhedrin therefore had to hand Jesus over to the Roman authorities.

Pontius Pilate was the Roman governor of Judea, the southern part of Israel. The Sanhedrin told him Jesus claimed to be the Messiah, the king of

the Jews. This was a religious crime for them, but that would not have worried Pilate. What did worry him was that it was a political crime as well. If it were true, Jesus would be claiming to be a rival king to Tiberius Caesar, the Roman Emperor. This would be treason.

When Pilate asked Jesus, 'Are you the king of the Jews?' he did not get a yes or no answer.

Jesus simply said, 'Those are your words, not mine.' He would not reply to the Jewish leaders' accusations. Pilate was astonished.

The Gospels say Pilate came to realize Jesus was innocent. At Passover time, the Roman governor used to release one prisoner, who was chosen by the people. So Pilate appealed to the crowd outside. A man called Barabbas was in prison as well as Jesus. Barabbas was a murderer, and may

have been a Zealot revolutionary. The Gospels say the Jewish authorities had stirred up the crowd against Jesus.

'Which one of these two do you want me to set free for you?' Pilate asked them.

'Barabbas!' the crowd shouted.

'What, then, shall I do with Jesus, called the Messiah?'

'Crucify him!' they answered. They carried on shouting it, and Pilate realized a riot was beginning. He passed sentence, and Jesus was condemned to death. He was to be executed by crucifixion. *Facts About The Crucifixion:-*

Crucifixion was slow, and horribly painful. The Romans crucified thousands of people. The routine was usually the same.

The criminal was stripped and whipped by the soldiers. This flogging caused terrible injuries. When Pilate's soldiers flogged Jesus, they mocked him

This stone is inscribed with Pontius Pilate's name. It comes from the time of Jesus. We know quite a lot about him. Philo and Josephus, two first-century Jewish writers, give us a lot of information.

He was governor (*procurator* or *prefect*) of Judea between AD26 and 36.

When he first came to Jerusalem, he brought some Roman military standards with him. These had pictures of the emperor on them. This broke the Jewish Law (Torah), and the Jews begged him

to take them away. He refused, and threatened to kill the Jews when they demonstrated. When he realized they would prefer to die, he gave in.

Pilate decided to build an aqueduct to improve the water supply. He took some of the Temple funds to pay for it. The Jews complained, and he had them beaten up.

Pilate once thought people on a religious journey (pilgrimage) were actually rioters. So he slaughtered them.

Pilate's time as prefect ended when he was summoned to Rome to explain his behaviour.

Now you have read this, what kind of a man do you think Pilate was?

too. They made him a crown out of thorns, gave him a purple cloak, and saluted him. 'Hail, king of the Jews,' they jeered.

They tied the horizontal beam of the cross to his arms, and led him through the streets, past the watching crowds. They hung a label round his neck, which would later be fixed to the cross. It gave his name, and his crime: 'Jesus of Nazareth, the king of the Jews.' Jesus was now too weak to carry the beam, and they forced a man in the crowd to help. His name was Simon of Cyrene.

They came to the place of execution. It was called Golgotha or Calvary, which means the Place of the Skull. Someone offered Jesus a painkiller, but he refused it. They nailed his wrists to the crossbeam. Then they hoisted it up, and fixed it to the heavy wooden stake set in the ground. Then his feet were nailed.

Two criminals were crucified with him. People shouted abuse. 'Save yourself, if you are the king of the Jews! Come down from the cross!'

One of the criminals joined in. 'Save yourself—and us.'

The other told him to be quiet. 'Don't you fear God?' he said. 'You received the same sentence he did. Ours, however, is only right, because we are getting what we deserve for what we did; but he has done no wrong.' He turned to the man who was dying with them. 'Remember me, Jesus, when you come as king.'

'Truly I say to you,' Jesus said, 'today you shall be with me in Paradise.'

Jesus hung on the cross for some hours. Then he cried out, 'My God, my God, why have you abandoned me?' Moments later, he was dead.

His death was watched by the centurion, the Roman officer who led the execution squad. 'Truly,' he said, 'this man was the Son of God.'

Jesus' body was buried in a tomb just outside Jerusalem. The tomb was paid for by Joseph of Arimathea, a member of the Sanhedrin who was one of Jesus' followers.

The suffering and death of Jesus are at the heart of Christianity.

Christians believe that God is absolutely good—perfect. But human beings are not. People do wrong and evil things (sins), so there is a 'barrier' between people and God. God intended people to enjoy his friendship, but that relationship has been broken.

In Jesus' time, the Jews thought animal sacrifices could take away their nation's sins—the animals died instead of the people. The first Christians used this idea to explain Jesus' death. As a result, Christians have always believed that Jesus' death was the *perfect* sacrifice: that Jesus died to take away the sins of the *whole world*. The barrier between God and human beings has been removed. People will still do evil things, but Jesus has died for them, so they can now find God's forgiveness and acceptance. Jesus has opened the way for them to reach God.

There are a number of different ideas, and pictures in the Bible, of how this works. The important thing is that Christians believe that Jesus was God, and that on the cross God dealt with evil in the world. He gave himself, as he wants us to give ourselves, for others. Jesus' death has drawn the sting from dying, because it is no longer the end of everything.

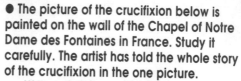

● Look up what Jesus said when he was dying. These are the Gospel references:

    Mark 15:34
    Luke 23:34 and 23:46
    John 19:30

Why do you think he says these things?

● Luke's Gospel says Jesus was also tried by Herod Antipas, who ruled the northern territory of Galilee for the Romans. Read this in Luke 23:8–12.

● The picture of the crucifixion below is painted on the wall of the Chapel of Notre Dame des Fontaines in France. Study it carefully. The artist has told the whole story of the crucifixion in the one picture.

Write a list of everything that is happening in the painting. (You can look up what the Gospels say to help you. See Mark 15:22–39; Luke 23:32–49; John 19:18–37.)

● We have already asked you to interview some Christians about important ideas. This time, try to ask a Christian priest or minister what Jesus' death means. He or she will have studied the idea, and should have some interesting things to say.

29

He is Risen!

Imagine how Jesus' disciples must have felt after his burial. He had been their friend. They had left everything to follow him, and for three years they had been with him. They had heard him preach to the crowds and seen people healed by him. They thought he was the Messiah, and had listened to his teaching with such hopes!

Now it was all over. Jesus was dead. One of their own number had betrayed him to his enemies. Very few of them had been brave enough to stay with him until the end. Most of them had panicked and run away, trying to save their own necks. Peter had even denied knowing him. As if all this was not bad enough, Jerusalem was full of people. The crowds who had demanded Jesus' crucifixion were still about. It was dangerous.

One by one the disciples began to drift back together again. What do you think they would have talked about? The Gospels do not tell us. What would have been going through their minds?

Write a poem about the disciples after Jesus' death.

Jesus' disciples were afraid and upset, but there were still things which had to be done. When people died it was usual to anoint their bodies with sweet-smelling spices. This was an act of love, as well as a religious duty. John's Gospel says that Joseph of Arimathea and Nicodemus had managed to anoint Jesus' corpse before putting it in Joseph's tomb, but Jesus' other followers do not seem to have known this. The women disciples set out as

119

early as they could to bring spices to the tomb.

Jesus died on a Friday afternoon. The next day was a Sabbath, when no work could be done—and that included anointing dead bodies. So the earliest time the women could go to Jesus' corpse was at daybreak on Sunday. The Gospels say that is what they did.

Jesus' tomb was in a garden. It was carved out of the rock, and had a large stone rolled over the entrance to close it once he had been buried. This was a common way of burying bodies in those days. Archaeologists have discovered quite a number of similar ones in and around Jerusalem.

The Gospels say that as the women got close to the tomb, they saw something which frightened and upset them. The stone was rolled away from its entrance. Jesus' tomb was open.

On the first Easter morning, so the Gospels tell us, Jesus' disciples found the great stone that had sealed the tomb of Jesus rolled back and the body gone—not stolen, but raised to life! This picture of a first-century tomb re-creates the atmosphere of that momentous dawn discovery.

What happened next is a bit confused. John's Gospel says that Mary Magdalene ran to Peter and John to tell them that somebody had stolen Jesus' body. Peter and John then ran to the tomb, and Peter went inside. Sure enough, Jesus' corpse had gone. Only his grave clothes were there.

Peter and John went back to where they were staying, but Mary stayed in the garden. She was terribly upset, and as she wept she saw two figures in white, sitting where the body of Jesus had been. John's Gospel says they were angels.

'Why are you crying?' they asked her.

'They have taken my Lord away,' she replied, 'and I do not know where they have put him.' Something made Mary turn round then, and she saw a man standing nearby.

'Woman, why are you weeping?' he asked her. Mary guessed he was the gardener—perhaps he had something to do with what had happened.

'Sir,' she said, 'if you took him away, tell me where you have put him, and I will go and get him.' The man looked at her.

'Mary!' he said. It was not the gardener at all. It was Jesus. He had risen from the dead.

● What did Mary originally think had happened to Jesus' body? Why did this upset her?

Jesus' rising from the dead is called his **resurrection**. In the next chapter we shall look at some more reports of the risen Jesus meeting his followers.

The resurrection is a very important belief for Christians. They would say that it is absolutely central to their faith and the way they understand the world. It was very important to the first Christians. The disciples certainly believed that they had met and spoken with Jesus personally after his resurrection.

For Jesus' followers, the resurrection meant four special things:

● It turned their *failure* and *despair* into *joy*. God had not abandoned Jesus after all!

● It showed that what they had started to believe was true. Jesus was everything they had thought him to be. The things he told them must have been true as well.

● God had acted in a powerful way in raising Jesus from the dead. Something very important indeed had happened: something which would change the world.

● Jesus had been raised to a *new sort of life*. He had not come back to this one. He would not live on earth and die again. He was not a ghost, either. In some astonishing way he had entered the Kingdom of God, and he was offering to share this new sort of life with everybody. His resurrection showed that he had overcome death, not just for himself but for everyone who followed him.

● Make a wall display showing what the resurrection meant to the earliest Christians. You could do this as a 'spider' diagram, using a picture or collage of the empty tomb as a background, and inventing appropriate illustrations for each point.

● How do Christians celebrate Jesus' resurrection today? Do some research into the festival of Easter. You could use your school or public library, but don't be afraid to ask for information from people you think might be able to help you as well.

30
Follow Me

The very first Christians were convinced that Jesus was raised from death and appeared to his disciples. This was the start of Christianity. Christians have believed it ever since.

The reports of the risen Jesus meeting his followers are therefore very important. When Jesus was crucified, the disciples were thrown into panic and despair. The Gospels say the meetings with the risen Jesus changed everything.

We now study three reports of these meetings.

● In the first, some of Jesus followers begin to understand why he died. They start to discover *what Jesus means*.
● In the second, they finally realize *who Jesus is*.
● In the third, they find out how their lives will change. They are told *what they have to do*.

Let's look at these in turn.

THE FIRST REPORT
(Luke's Gospel, 24:13–35)

Two of Jesus' followers were walking to the village of Emmaus, near Jerusalem. On their way, they were joined by a stranger. He asked them what they were talking about.

One of them, Cleopas, answered sadly,

'Are you the only visitor in Jerusalem who doesn't know the things that have been happening there these last few days?'

'What things?' the stranger asked.

'The things that happened to Jesus of Nazareth,' came the reply. They explained about the crucifixion, and that his tomb was found to be empty. There were even rumours that he was alive.

The stranger told them it all had to happen that way. The Messiah had to suffer before he could enter his glory. He explained how it fitted in with what the Old Testament said. It was planned by God.

As they arrived at the village, the stranger looked as though he meant to walk on further. 'Stay with us,' they suggested. 'The day is almost over, and it is getting dark.'

The stranger sat down to eat with them. It was not until he asked God's blessing on the bread and broke it that they realized who he was.

When they looked round, Jesus was gone.

THE SECOND REPORT
(John's Gospel, 20:19–29)

The disciples were meeting in secret behind locked doors. They were frightened. This is hardly surprising. The Jewish authorities or the Romans could come looking for them at any time.

Suddenly, Jesus was there. 'Peace be with you,' he said. The disciples were astonished to see him, but overjoyed as well.

Jesus spoke again. 'As the Father sent me, so I send you.' He breathed on them and said, 'Receive the Holy Spirit.' He gave them the authority to forgive people's sins.

Thomas, however, was not with them. When the other disciples met him later, they told him what had happened. Thomas did not believe a word of it. 'Unless I see the scars of the nails in his hands and put my finger on those scars and my hand in his side, I will not believe,' he said.

A week later, Jesus appeared to them again. He told Thomas to touch his wounds. 'Stop your doubting, and believe!'

Thomas recognized Jesus, and realized, too, who Jesus really was: 'My Lord, and my God!'

'Do you believe because you see me?' Jesus asked. 'Blessed are those who have not seen me, but believe all the same.'

The disciples gather round: Jesus, their teacher, has so much to tell them.

THE THIRD REPORT
(John's Gospel, 21:1–24)

Some time later, a number of the disciples were fishing on Lake Galilee. They worked all night, but did not catch a thing.

At dawn, they noticed Jesus standing on the shore, although they did not yet recognize him. 'Have you caught anything?' he called across to them.

'Nothing,' they answered.

'Throw your net out on the right side of the boat,' he said.

When they did so, they had such an enormous catch that the nets nearly broke. John realized who the man was. 'It is the Lord!' he exclaimed to Peter, who immediately jumped overboard and swam ashore to meet Jesus. The others followed in the boat.

Jesus was grilling some fish over a fire. 'Come and eat,' he said.

When they had finished breakfast, Jesus turned to Peter. 'Simon, son of John,' he said, 'do you love me?'

'Yes, Lord,' he answered, 'you know that I love you.'

Jesus asked the question three times, each time telling Peter that he had to look after Jesus' followers: 'Take care of my sheep.'

Peter had completely let Jesus down, but now he was forgiven. He and the other disciples had a job to do. Jesus repeated what he had said to them when he called them to be his disciples: 'Follow me.' Jesus told Peter he would follow him to the death. Like his master, Peter would die by crucifixion.

When Peter asked what would happen to John, Jesus said he did not need to worry about that. After all, Peter had been told what to do.

'Follow me.'

Answer these questions in sentences.

THE FIRST REPORT
● Where were Jesus' followers going?
● What were they talking about?
● What did Jesus explain to them?
● When did they recognize him?

THE SECOND REPORT
● Why were the disciples meeting behind locked doors?
● What did Jesus say to them?
● What did he give them authority to do?
● Which disciple was not there?
● What did this disciple call Jesus?

THE THIRD REPORT
● Where were the disciples fishing?
● What did Jesus tell them to do with the nets?

● Which disciple recognized Jesus?
● Which disciple swam ashore to meet him?
● After breakfast, what did Jesus ask Peter?
● What did Jesus tell Peter to do?

There are some points to notice in these reports from the Gospels.
● In the first report, Jesus' followers recognize him just at the moment when he breaks the bread.
● In the second report, Jesus says, 'Blessed are those who have not seen me, but believe all the same.'
● In the third report, Jesus tells his disciples, 'Follow me.'

These points are important to the Gospel writers and their Christian readers. Try to work out why.

EPILOGUE
The Story Continues

The New Testament says the risen Jesus appeared to the disciples for about forty days.

When he met them by Lake Galilee, he told them again, 'Follow me.' At their final meeting with him he explained what would happen:

> 'When the Holy Spirit comes upon you, you will be filled with power, and you will be witnesses for me in Jerusalem, in all Judea and Samaria, and to the ends of the earth.' (Acts 1:8)

The last meeting is described in the Acts of the Apostles. (Acts is volume two of Luke's Gospel, although it is printed after John's Gospel in the Bible.) Acts uses picture language to describe what happened:

● A *cloud* surrounded Jesus. The Old Testament writers thought that when

God appeared, he appeared in a cloud. When Acts says a cloud surrounded Jesus, it means that God is at work.

● Jesus *'went up'* or *'ascended'* into heaven. This does not mean he took off like a rocket! We use picture language like this as well. If you say, 'I am going up the road,' you do not expect to have to put on a space suit! Acts means that Jesus 'went up' to the 'place' where God the Father is.

Jesus had gone away, but he had left the disciples with two things:

● A promise. They would be filled with the Holy Spirit.
● An instruction. They had to spread the news about Jesus, everywhere.

Acts says the *promise* came true soon afterwards. Jesus' followers were

Christians believe that God continues to work through his people today, using their different gifts and personalities to express his life-changing message to people everywhere. Some are well-known—like athlete Kriss Akabusi and singer Cliff Richard. Others, like this Indian nurse who cares for the blind, are not. But all share Jesus' commission to make him known and draw strength from his promise to be with them always.

meeting together on the Jewish festival of Pentecost. Suddenly they had an extraordinary and overwhelming experience of the power of God. This was so powerful that Acts says it was like a rushing wind and tongues of fire. The disciples ran out into the streets. Crowds of people were gathered in the city from all over the world, speaking different languages. The disciples began to preach to them about Jesus. There was a miracle. Everybody could

understand them. This was the Holy Spirit at work.

Christians believe that God the Holy Spirit still works through the church—the people of God—today.

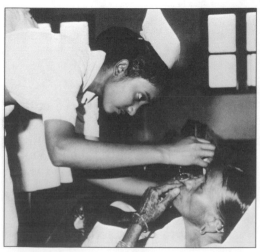

At the feast of Whitsun, they look back to when it all started with the apostles.

Jesus' instruction to spread the news about him was carried out by his followers. The message soon spread through the Roman Empire. Jesus' followers began to be called 'Christians'. Christian communities (or *churches*) were set up in major cities. They were started by missionaries.

Paul was one of the most important of these missionaries. He had begun by hating the new movement. He even did his best to stamp it out, travelling from city to city and throwing Christians in prison. But in about AD36, everything changed for him. In an extraordinary way, he met the risen Jesus. He became a Christian, and dedicated the rest of his life to spreading the message about Jesus.

There are over one thousand million Christians, of every race and colour, around the world today, and there have been countless others down the centuries. Christians try to follow Jesus' teaching. They look forward to being with him in heaven. And they remember

the promise of the risen Jesus, at the end of Matthew's Gospel:

'I am always with you:
to the end of time.'

Index